The Business Plan Guide for Independent Consultants

The Business Plan
Guide for
Independent Consultants

Herman Holtz

JOHN WILEY & SONS, INC.
New York • Chichester • Brisbane • Toronto • Singapore

This text is printed on acid-free paper.

This publication is designed to provide accurate and authoritative
information in regard to the subject matter covered. It is sold
with the understanding that the publisher is not engaged in
rendering legal, accounting, or other professional services.
If legal advice or other expert assistance is required, the services
of a competent professional person should be sought.

Note: A computer diskette is contained in the cloth edition,
ISBN 0-471-59736-8.

REQUIREMENTS:
An IBM® PC family computer or compatible computer with 256K
minimum memory, a 3.5 " high-density floppy drive, PC DOS, MS
DOS, or DR DOS Version 2.0 or later, and a printer.

Library of Congress Cataloging-in-Publication Data:

Holtz, Herman.
    The business plan guide for independent consultants/Herman Holtz.
        p.   cm.
    Includes index.
    ISBN 0-471-59736-8 (cloth).—ISBN 0-471-59735-X (paper)
        1. Business consultants.   2. Consulting—Vocational guidance.
    I. Title.
    HD69.C6H6185   1994
    658.4'6—dc20   94-6924

Printed in the United States of America

10 9 8 7 6 5 4 3

Preface

In one sense, everyone in business, from the smallest to the largest enterprise, started with a business plan. At its smallest size, the business plan is in the entrepreneur's head and may be no more detailed than a general idea to sell a product, sometimes as yet undefined. Other times there are thick, many-paged projections and detailed provisions in writing for incorporation, funding, staffing, marketing, and all the other details, such as lists of suppliers and carefully defined prospective customers. Amazingly often, however, messages such as the following appear in CompuServe and other small-business forums, addressed to "ALL": "I want to start a business from my home, and I am looking for ideas. What should I sell? How do I get started?"

Sometimes the focus is just a bit sharper, but still pretty vague, as in the following typical example: "I taught myself to program in 'C' and I want to become a computer consultant now. I am looking for suggestions. How do I find clients and what should I charge them?"

These are not exaggerations. Such messages appear daily on computer bulletin boards. Many reveal that the common definition of a "consultant" as someone with special experience and expertise has become lost somehow. One individual wanted to start a practice as a cost consultant to help companies reduce their overhead, but wanted suggestions on how to go about learning how to reduce overhead and control costs. Another inquirer was a woman who wanted suggestions for learning computer programming so she could become a consultant overnight. From beginning student to expert consultant in one easy leap!

I get telephone calls and letters from readers asking just such questions. In fact, I had a call recently from someone who heard me speak at a writer's group about custom writing for clients. She had started her business, won her first client, and wanted to know what to charge. She was asking everyone she could reach for an estimate of average writing production—for example, the number of pages per day upon which to base her estimates in quoting prices to new clients.

Fortunately, most beginning freelance writers, like most beginning independent consultants, start by working from home with little or no initial investment. Were they to make a substantial investment with no more preparation than these examples illustrate, they might very well lose their investment quite quickly.

The sad truth is that the odds are very much against these individuals being successful. They decide to start or have started a business with a complete lack of thought or planning. And yet, although these represent extreme cases of lack of preparedness for business, by far the majority of independent consultants enter into practice with not much more preparation and planning than this.

A business plan should be developed before the business is launched. The idea is to do the research and make all the plans before venturing. This book is necessarily based on the premise that you are doing just that or planning to do so. However, I know that you may have begun your practice without organized planning, as many do, and came later to the realization that there are great advantages in having a sound business plan on paper. If so, some of the material in this book, especially in the early pages, will come as no news to you, but it is necessary to include it here.

As Mark Twain observed about the weather, everyone talks about it—the need for a business plan, that is—but most people starting and running small businesses (70 percent, according to one business poll) do nothing about it. At least, not until later, after they discover that it might have been helpful to have a plan, prepare for the unexpected, and have measures ready to cope with it. The excuses given, according to David H. "Andy" Bangs, a widely quoted expert on the subject, are numerous—for example, "My business is unique," "I haven't any competition," and "I'm bad with numbers," are among those most frequently heard. A complicating factor is that not everyone means the same thing by the term *business plan*; it has more than one meaning—five or more meanings or levels of meaning, in fact, as Dr. Joseph R. Mancuso points out in his book, *How to Write a Winning Business Plan* (Prentice-Hall, 1985). The phrase *business plan* is often a euphemism, actually referring to a loan application, funding proposal, or prospectus for prospective investors. What we are interested in here is a start-up and operating guide. Syndicated small business columnist Jane Applegate confirmed in a recent column that many and perhaps even most business owners are unaware that there are two general types of business plans. These are characterized by business plan consultant Molly Thorpe of Canoga Park, California, as "financing plans" and "focusing plans." (Yes, there are a number of business plan consultants, some of whom you will meet later in these pages.)

There are many how-to books on the subject of writing business plans. In fact, the number is surprisingly high. There are also quite a few consultants who specialize in helping clients write business plans, and even some who run entire seminars on the subject. It seems strange that there should be so many business plan experts writing, lecturing, and consulting on the subject, and still so many businesses operate without a business plan and apparently are indifferent to a need for such an instrument. On the other hand, it is understandable that the independent consultant—that harried individual addressed here—might be immediately intimidated by the existing books: Most appear to be addressed to the executives of the large corporations with multimillion-dollar programs and problems. Few present guidance suitable for the small, independent practitioner, and none that I could find are geared specifically to independent consultants, nor to other independent professionals facing similar business problems. There seems to me to be a clearly evident need for guidance that is addressed to the independent consultant, based on an in-depth understanding of the typical business problems and specific needs of independent consultants.

A reasonable first step, therefore, is to take some of the mystery out of the subject, for it does seem to be rather mysterious to the uninitiated, especially to the beginning entrepreneur. That might well start by getting an accurate—and that means hard-headed—perspective on what the business plan is and is not, beginning with that broad distinction into the two classes already noted, in terms of *why* it is useful to have a business plan and what it is intended to do for *you* (never mind anyone else).

HERMAN HOLTZ

Wheaton, Maryland
July 1994

Contents

Introduction 1

1. Why You Need a Business Plan 7

What Is a Business Plan? / For Whom Is the Plan Written? / The Basic Elements / A Major Reason for Writing a Business Plan / How Big Should a Business Plan Be?

2. Mission Statements and Business Definitions 25

Making a Start / What Business Are You In? / Developing Your Business Definitions / The Final Mission Statement / One Mission Statement or Several?

3. Start-Up Planning 47

The Importance of a Good Beginning / Services to Offer / Business Location / Business Organization / Choosing a Business Name / Furniture, Fixtures, Equipment, and Supplies / Basic Marketing Materials / Administrative Considerations / Short-Term Goals and Objectives / Estimate of Start-Up Costs / Now, the Nitty-Gritty

4. Initial Commitments   **59**

The Form of Organization: Choices and
Considerations / Side Effects of Decisions /
Planning the Next Phase

5. Market Analysis   **79**

The Ultimate Niche Market: Too Good to Be
True? / Who Will Be Your Clients? / Identify the
Service / Identify the Clients / A Word About the
Worksheets

**6. Analyzing and Qualifying Markets
and Segments**   **95**

Qualifying Your Prospects / Qualifying Your
Markets and Niches / Refining Your Analysis /
Designing the Database

7. The Marketing Plan   **111**

The Marketing Process / A Marketable Service /
Reaching Your Market / Next, the "How To"

**8. Planning the Presentations and
Using the Tools**   **127**

It Is a Matter of Presentation / What Motivates
a Prospect to Become a Client? / Using Your
Sales Tools

9. Zeroing in on Your Market   **145**

Market Research Versus Market Intelligence /
Gathering Market Intelligence

10. Rates and Pricing   **159**

The Basic Variables / Establishing a Pricing
Policy / What Your Rate Should Include

11. The Financial Side of the Business   171

The Music of the Numbers / Accounting Systems /
The Need for Start-Up Capital / Working Capital /
Income Projections / Cash Needs Calculation /
Summarizing Your Financial Data / Where to Go
from Here

12. A Sample Business Plan   203

Appendix: References and Resources   213

Index   219

User Information   223

Introduction

Writing a business plan is not easy. Writing about how to write a business plan is also not easy. I know of no other how-to-write subject—for example, how to write a report, how to write a proposal, or how to write a resume—that relies to such a great extent on lengthy outlines, or even uses outlines other than very sketchy and informal ones. Why is learning the art of business-plan writing so dependent on highly detailed outlines? Perhaps it is because many of those who write on the subject assume automatically that "business plan" is a synonym for "loan application" or "investment prospectus."

Outlines for business plans abound; it's incredibly easy to find one. And when you do find one, you have probably found all of them. They tend to have the same general format and approach, especially those that are plainly aimed directly at the raising of capital in some manner. We will soon be covering in some detail what a business plan is but for now I wish to enter the outline route as a preview of—preparation for—what is to come. I will not, however, subject you to one of those outlines that runs on for several pages in stultifying detail. I don't think it necessary, especially since the raising of capital is presumably a minor key for most, if not all, readers of this book.

You'll see on the next page a somewhat truncated business plan outline—the details of which are discussed in much greater length in chapters to follow. It is a rather short outline compared with many others, but those tend to be directed to planning large companies,

The Bobtailed Business Plan Outline

- Mission statement
    Define the business you're in
    Include the essence of your business strategy
- Start-up capital requirement
- Start-up decisions
    Office location (home, office building, other)
    Starting fixtures, furniture, equipment, and supplies required
    Specific services to be offered to clients
    Short- and long-term goals and objectives (size, capability, and sales volume)
- Marketing plan
    Profile of typical clients/prospective clients
    Competition anticipated, kind of number (suggestions for analyzing)
    Advertising requirements and costs (full analysis)
    Promotions planned and costs (full analysis)
- Rate structure
    Basis (daily, hourly, fixed price, and so on)
    Rates (discussions and suggestions)
- Potential for diversification/other profit centers
    Related services (examples and suggestions)
    Products (examples and suggestions)
- Contingency plans
    Alternative services/products, if and as necessary (suggestions)
    Alternative markets, if and as necessary (extended discussion)
- Income projections (suggested analytical methods)

often manufacturing entities, as well as to raising capital for major ventures. Our principal concern here is to develop a business plan for the successful building and operation of an independent consulting venture.

The mission statement.   The mission statement, also known by other names such as "purpose" and "description," may seem somewhat pointless since it should state, as simply as possible (only a sentence or two for even a fairly large organization), what the overall goal of the business is. Many read simply, "Joe's Hoagie Shop will provide the most delicious and generous hoagies at competitive prices," or "The Equal Opportunity Services Corporation is dedicated to providing quality financial services of all kinds for the entire community, through a highly trained and well-qualified staff of professionals."

Neither statement says or contributes much. A mission statement should say more than some obvious platitude that is more reflective of wishful thinking than of real analysis of what the projected business is to be all about. A proper mission statement should provide a raison d'être, preferably as some well thought out strategy. It ought to be, in fact, a definition of the business that distinguishes it in some important way. Pete's Hamburger Stand is obviously in business to sell hamburgers, but what is Pete's strategy for making his hamburger stand successful? (See Chapter 2 for sample statements.)

The start-up capital requirement.   Every business plan addresses the subject of capital—finances. The more you review sample business plans, how-to books on the subject, and software programs that do much of the work for you in building a business plan, the more conscious you become of the emphasis on financing (see Chapter 11). It is a premise of this book that you, the typical independent consultant, do not require outside financing. Still, it is possible that yours may be the exception—a consultancy that requires substantial initial investment. But even if you do not require more financing than you can write your own check for, you won't know that without thinking it out objectively, and certainly you ought to know just what you will need, even if the amount is small. You can't know what that amount it is to be without analysis and planning. This is the place to do that.

Start-up decisions.   The decisions necessary to start-up represent quite another matter. You do, indeed, need to make choices about where to establish your office and what services you will offer clients, two of the most basic and most critical decisions that are interrelated. Most independent consultants find it possible to start from an office in their home and many remain in an office at home permanently. However, it may be the case that you need more room or facilities than you can manage in a home office. You must decide what you will need, not by random guessing but by careful analysis. You should also be projecting a few initial estimates here on your goals and objectives vis-à-vis the size of your practice and sales volume you anticipate, and how those objectives relate to your decisions. Remember, most of these decisions are necessarily tentative at this point. (See Chapter 3 for details.)

Marketing plan.   If there is any element of your consulting practice that needs clear and level-headed planning, it is marketing. You can probably manage without outside financing; you can keep your own books, even if you do a clumsy job of it; you can keep indifferent records of all kinds; you can use almost any kind of computer and other office equipment, even if it is not the most practical or most efficient system for you; and you can even be somewhat less than superb at whatever services you provide clients. You can be deficient in all these areas and other ways and still survive, perhaps even prosper, if you have enough clients—enough *sales.* You cannot survive long without enough sales. Hence, we will spend a good bit of time discussing planning for this most important (and often most difficult) function of your business: winning clients and managing the growth of your venture. It is a complex subject, requiring identification of typical clients and prospective clients (Chapter 5), analysis of competition, evaluation of market segments (Chapter 6), and consideration of advertising and promotional activities (Chapters 7 and 8), among other things. When thinking about your marketing plans, you should also take the time to consider and plan to establish proper marketing databases (see in Chapter 6), for they need to be planned ahead and built carefully over time.

Rate structure. Many consultants find fee setting difficult. How to charge clients and how much to charge them can be baffling. Eavesdrop on consultants exchanging messages on any electronic bulletin board system (BBS), where eavesdropping is called "lurking"(and it's perfectly respectable to do so because these are public forums, open to all users of the BBS), and you will hear many discussions and exchanges of opinions on this subject. Most newcomers to consulting have a difficult time finding a rate that they believe clients will pay, and thus many completely underrate their worth. (Everybody seems to believe that their area is one in which clients will not pay normal rates, but insist on getting bargains.) Advance planning (see Chapter 10) will help establish in your own mind the rightness of the rates you decide on and combat the fear of alienating and losing clients by asking a fair price for your services.

Potential for diversification and other profit centers. This is a most important subject, closely related to marketing, and in many cases critical to survival. Most businesses have six seasons, the four seasons of the year and the slow and busy seasons, which are unrelated to the annual seasons. They may occur at any time and more than once during the year. Consulting is not an exception. The difficulty is in building enough reserves during the busy seasons to carry you through the slow seasons. It is not easy for a one-person enterprise to do that, and the establishment of complementing income centers is a method many have used successfully to overcome the problem of the slow seasons. Actually, the several methods complement each other so well, in most cases, that they often can become integrated in a system that is greater than the sum of its parts. The time to project needs and prepare for them is now—in the business planning process.

Products are part of this planning but they need to be planned as specific items. They do not spring from your forehead spontaneously but must be well thought out and planned. Doing so now, as part of your business plan, will pay off in benefits later. Here, you will consider all the products and correlate these ideas with those of diversification and ancillary income centers.

Contingency plans.   The most carefully laid plans succumb all too often to the well-known Murphy's Law, which predicts in its essence that anything that can go wrong will do so. With that amply warranted assumption firmly established, it is logical to expect and provide for contingencies. Plans for alternatives should be prepared and placed on the shelf, ready to be summoned to the rescue if the need arises.

Income projections.   Finally, we come to the last item in this bobtailed outline (which is condensed only in the details, for all major items and areas of coverage are specified and will be discussed in detail as we go, especially in Chapter 11). These figures, which ought to be estimated as chronological segments, based on anticipated growth of your practice, must correlate with your other estimates of sales and rates. Each element serves as a check on the others and helps achieve realistic figures. The figures are then helpful in monitoring the development of your practice. They are milestones marking the way. However, they are also estimates. In fact, the first ones are usually "guesstimates" and ought to be so recognized. With a little experience to season your judgment, you will make much better projections when the time comes to review these first estimates and recast them.

One thing will become increasingly clear as we proceed: None of these items or concerns exists independently of the others. There is a relationship between all, and a direct relationship in some cases (for example, rate and income projections). The various estimates must be capable of logical integration. Changing estimates is likely to require a hard look at others that will be affected by the change. That becomes more and more the case as growing experience begins to replace early estimates with facts and temper estimates of what is yet to come.

The following chapters will help you to begin making such estimates in order to consider—and finally develop—your own business plan.

1

Why You Need a Business Plan

A few basic explanations of purpose are needed here to define the playing field, especially since the independent consultant's need for a business plan is almost always quite different from that of many others, such as manufacturers and retailers, especially in the matter of capital requirements.

WHAT IS A BUSINESS PLAN?

If you are to be urged to write a business plan, and to read a whole book on the subject, it seems fair to define the term first. That is easy to do, and yet not so easy. One problem is the same as that of defining consulting itself: There are too many definitions, and they are all both correct and incorrect, according to the application. The simple, generalized definition of a business plan is easy enough, however. It does not provide great insight, but it will do as a start. Linda Elkins, a business plan consultant in Annapolis, Maryland, who offers a business plan writing service, opens her definition of the business plan with this simple statement:

A business plan is the clear summation of a company's goals, the plans to reach those goals, the resources they will use along the

7

way, and the measurements they will make to show they have reached the goals.

Another specialist in writing business plans, Marcia Layton, president of Layton & Co. in Rochester, New York, says much the same thing in introducing the subject. She makes a special point of the need for the plan to be on paper:

> A business plan does *not* exist solely in someone's head. A business plan exists only when it is communicated on paper, so that others (such as financial advisors, attorneys, accountants, and, most importantly, employees) can react to and discuss the organization's plans and objectives.

These are brief and introductory definitions, of course, and are stated in such general terms as to say very little. Those two business plan specialists I quote here have a great deal more to say on the subject, and we'll get to that later. You will see that fully defining a business plan requires describing what goes into it, and that, in turn, varies according to the nature of the business, the overall aims of the consultant (it *is* for consultants—for you—that this book is written), and the individual circumstances of each case. Thus, some of what you will find written here is universally true and can be applied to any and all business plans and business situations, but a great deal of it is relevant to consultants only and to individual situations. Thus, there is a hazard in generalizing too freely. What is right and necessary for John Jefferson in planning and running his security consulting practice is not what is right and necessary for Charlene Chambers in conducting her computer consulting business. That, too, should become more apparent as we proceed and learn not only what a business plan is but what it must do for you, and why you need it.

FOR WHOM IS THE PLAN WRITTEN?

In the two brief and simplified definitions of a business plan given at the beginning of this chapter, no mention is made of the matter of finances. That omission is deliberate because it is one of the major differences between this book and other books and programs on the subject. There will be more references to finances—you will be reminded of this—as we continue, but take note that while the business plans we will discuss here will not and can not ignore accounting, budgeting, and financial considerations, they will be developed to help you succeed in building and running your practice successfully as their main objective. That is, they will be written for *you* and for any business consultants and counselors you may retain—for example, accountants, lawyers, and professional marketers—not for bankers or investors.

THE BASIC ELEMENTS

One could come up with a lengthy laundry list of information that ought to be in a business plan. In reviewing some of the abundant literature available on the subject, I found a great many terms used, such as "basic business concept." I was not sure just what that meant; it could mean almost anything. I found, too, that there are items considered to be necessary for all business plans, but not all appeared to be justified for the independent consultant. The requirement to identify the location of the business is one such item. I am sure this is a major consideration for many kinds of business, but it does not appear to me to be a concern for the independent consultant, at least not in the ordinary or typical case. Nor does the requirement to identify the number and types of personnel appear to be pertinent to the establishment and operation of a one-person consulting practice. (It may become a concern eventually, if you grow in size, but we consider here the sole operator consultancy.) And, finally, we have already decided that the matter of financing is a secondary concern here, and so I will defer discussing it entirely until much later, when I will offer some coverage of that subject for the exceptional case.

You may decide, now or later, to offer seminars, other training, a newsletter, special reports, or other special items that may or may not involve products. I consider these to be part of consulting—they are additional ways of making your expert knowledge and skills available to support client needs—and so your business plan may include these initially or have them added later.

On that premise—that we will plan the consulting services only, and include such ancillary activities as those just mentioned to be also consulting services—I suggest six areas of concern to consider, analyze, and plan for:

1. A general definition of the business.
2. Specific services to be offered.
3. Definition(s) of market(s) you plan to address, with estimates of size and share you believe you can and should capture.
4. Your marketing plans and strategies, including especially competitive strategies.
5. Management and administrative plans for your venture.
6. Cost projections and estimated cash-flow needs.

A MAJOR REASON FOR WRITING A BUSINESS PLAN

One can come up with a great many reasons for writing a business plan, and you will find many of those reasons cited in these pages. You may find you need a communications tool that conveys your ideas, research, and plans to others, such as to a business counselor or a lawyer. You may feel that your principal need is for a guide to help you manage your business. You may want a yardstick by which to measure progress and evaluate changes. These are all legitimate reasons, and any may be the prime mover in urging you to write your business plan. The most important motive probably varies as widely as do the characteristics of different businesses and their owners. In my own view, the most compelling reason for having a business plan can be found in the casualty statistics of small business generally: The number of casualties is shockingly high, and the anecdotal examples of this unpleasant truth are as plentiful as are the statistics. Here is just one from my own observation:

I recently drove by a small strip shopping center that opened less than two years ago near my home. It had been a gasoline filling station that went out of business during the gasoline shortages, as did many service stations in that time. For years after it had been little more than an eyesore of a large vacant lot in the midst of a business district, where an enterprising individual sold Christmas trees in December. It was a good location at a busy intersection, big enough to accommodate a small bank and five retail stores, when a developer finally built the little shopping center. The bank and stores were leased and opened for business as soon as the construction was finished.

Now, less than two years later, I was struck by the fact that only the bank anchoring one end of the strip was the original occupant; every other business there was a replacement of the first ones that had opened when the shopping center started. Every one of the original businesses, other than the bank, had foundered here, and new businesses had taken over the spaces.

It's rather typical. By far the majority of new small businesses do not survive their second year in business, and many do not survive the first year. Only after three to four years of survival can it be assumed that the business is likely to display a reasonable degree of longevity. Venture capitalists do not expect profits from firms they capitalize until after three to four years of existence, and consider the achievement of breakeven operation in those early years to be quite satisfactory. Even so, the failures are great in number. Success in business is almost invariably more difficult to achieve than people think when they try their own hands at it. We learn from experience, and experience is education, but it gives us the test first and the lesson afterward, as something known as Vernon Saunders Law first observed.

There are many reasons offered for disappointing business performances—that is, for the many business failures. Among them are inadequate financing, poor locations, poor purchasing practices, inadequate accounting, and poor management. But probably the most serious shortcoming is poor marketing: No business, large or small, can survive without an adequate share of the market—without sufficient sales. On the other hand, most businesses that enjoy adequate sales volume are able to survive other shortcomings that might otherwise be fatal weaknesses. (The harsh fact is that most businesses have weaknesses that would be fatal if the business did not do well enough in marketing, but the business survives its own faults because it brings in enough sales to tolerate a great many shortcomings. Anyone who has worked for a large corporation has observed the many inefficiencies and faults that the organization tolerates and is able to afford.)

As an independent consultant, you have a limited budget for such faults and weaknesses: You can't afford more than a few. You are particularly vulnerable to weak marketing. If you are a typical independent consultant, you probably have little to worry about with regard to location, purchasing, or financing for launching a new practice. Due to the inherent nature of consulting, especially independent consulting, these are usually not highly critical factors. You do not need expensive office locations or a great deal of equipment or inventory (consulting rarely requires extensive financing) and you probably do not need a secretary, at least not in the beginning. But you do need clients, and any serious shortcoming there is likely to be a fatal flaw.

One reason that marketing poses a special problem is that most clients do not go to great pains to seek out consultants. They will call in consultants usually recommended by their friends and associates, but will not make great efforts in quest of a consultant. In fact, the very thought of retaining a consultant may not even occur to most prospective clients if someone does not suggest it to them. It is the other way around: To win clients, you must seek out and pursue the them. Word of mouth may produce most of your business eventually, as many consultants claim, but that can't happen until you have "been around a while," and have built a reputation and a following. At least in the beginning, even for those fortunate enough to eventually get their business via word of mouth, marketing must be aggressive and proactive to be effective. By and large, new consultancies fail more because of the lack of sales—the fatal weakness of marketing—than because of any other factor. Far too many beginning consultants make no serious effort to mount a comprehensive marketing effort, or even know what that is. Instead, they tend to rely on a few personal contacts, chance, and word of mouth to generate business, at least in the beginning. (In fact, many base their decisions to launch themselves into an independent consulting venture on the promise of business from a personal contact or two.) Eventually, the slow season arrives, as it does in every business, even for the consultant who was swamped with orders in the beginning. Then the consultant who has not prepared and carried out a marketing plan or has otherwise prepared to cope with the inevitable business slowdown is in trouble immediately.

Preparing for the slow times is one compelling reason for having a business plan, but it is not the only one. There are many reasons for having a business plan as early in the venture as possible—most ideally, long before you hang out your shingle—while you are still in the contemplative stages of launching a new career as an independent consultant, all having a direct bearing on your success as an independent consultant. However, of all those other reasons, probably the most important is one you won't hear from the sobersides business experts who will go on an on about financing, inventory, accounting, and sundry other management concerns. It is Murphy's Law.

Anticipating Murphy's Law and Its Impact

There have been many Murphy's Laws offered over the years but the most basic premise, that upon which all Murphy's Laws are based, is that *anything that can go wrong will go wrong*—meaning that if left to themselves, all things will always go wrong. And, of course, they do— or it often seems that way. In any case, prevention of this occurrence requires that things not be left to themselves but that they be monitored and managed, continuously and without fail. No matter how carefully you plan, a disaster you did not anticipate, a disastrous circumstance you could not possibly control, an incredible fiasco that could only happen under the most exceptional and unlikely combination of circumstances, or a debacle that required the most unusual coincidence of misfortunes will happen every time. Exaggeration? Of course it is. It is exaggerated partly to be sardonically humorous and partly to stress the point by overstatement. It is wise to be prepared always for the curse of Murphy to strike with his monstrous laws, for the most unlikely and unpredictable disasters to happen, because that is what Murphy's Law is about.

Disasters are, of course, always unexpected. We don't plan misfortune, at least not consciously. In fact, all too often we don't really plan at all, in the deeper meaning of the word. What little planning we do is based on the assumption that all will be well. Thus, we tend more to improvise, expecting to hurdle or circumnavigate any obstacles that arise. The spontaneous remedies we rely on may work for the minor impedimenta we encounter along the way. Preventing and overcoming major calamities, however, requires something stronger, much stronger than casual troubleshooting, with duct tape and Elmer's glue remedies: They require careful and thorough advance planning.

Business plans are written always in the upbeat, optimistic mode, planning all the measures to make everything go right: That is the basic objective of writing the plan. But a truly effective business plan also provides remedies for things that do not go right.

On one occasion, the company of which I was the general manager contracted with a federal agency, the Air Pollution Control Office, forerunner of the Environmental Protection Agency (EPA), to produce a set of standards that were required by law. The need was so great (even Congress was growing impatient and pressing the agency to publish the standards, at long last), the agency even asked us to print the standards for them because they did not believe the Government Printing Office could produce the manuals before the deadline that had been mandated by Congress. That deadline required the manuals be in the mail and postmarked before the first day of the coming year.

Time was characteristically short and the printer who had sworn on his mother's memory and his father's honor that he would meet our deadlines without difficulty was obviously not going to be able to do it. And so we found ourselves on December 31 at the printer's place of business, with all the hands and feet, my own and all of those I could muster from my own shop, helping the printer assemble, bind, and package the manuals so that they could arrive at the main postoffice in time to get a December 31 postmark. It was a Faustian scene of desperate devils struggling on New Year's Eve with mysterious tasks of which we knew nothing. We made it, barely, through frantic efforts and good fortune, but I considered the circumstance a result of very bad planning, of course. I had put my faith on a very important contract in the hands of a local printer who made glib promises that he could not have kept, had I not paid my own workers overtime to help him do the job we were paying him to do. Had I done a proper job of contingency planning, I would have had better alternatives to that printer prepared as failsafe measures.

Business plans ought to include contingency planning. They usually do not because so often the focus is on creating a plan to support efforts to raise financing, and one does not want to point out to bankers, investors, or venture capitalists even the most remote possibility of cataclysmic events descending on the business. But let's not talk about financing yet. We want a business plan to minimize the probability of catastrophes and maximize the probability of recovering rapidly or surmounting the trouble at minimal cost and delay, should they happen nevertheless. It is unrealistic to ignore the possibility that such problems will arise when we know that they probably will. Whatever he was, Murphy was not a fool.

Let us hope that those calamitous circumstances never arise, while we recognize that they may. Let us hope that the possibility gives you pause and directs your attention to the matter at hand. And now that I have your attention, let's go on to the general considerations that you may not have pondered before now.

First of all, bear in mind that the business plan we are talking about here is for your own use only. It is not to be the basis for an effort to gather financing. You are not going to build a plan to present to a bank, a board of directors, or even to a group of associates; it is to be a plan to guide you around the shoals that most independent entrepreneurs have to maneuver, especially in the early years of building a business. If you present it to anyone, it will be to consultants you have retained to help you—legal, accounting, computer/dataprocessing, and/or marketing experts.

Not intending to use your plan to gain financial backing does not mean that it should be less complete or less detailed than it would otherwise be, but it should be informal and highly flexible. Your primary objective in writing a business plan is to increase the probability of conducting your venture successfully by anticipating needs and problems and being prepared to cope with them. That will be the orientation throughout these pages.

Charting Your Course

As the employee of an organization, large or small, you were a specialist. You were hired because of some special skill and related experience, and you had a certain job to do every day related to and depending on that special skill. You might have been diverted occasionally to some corollary chore, but most of the time you did that special job for which you were hired.

Now, as an independent consultant, you see yourself as more the specialist than ever, even the superspecialist. As a direct-marketing specialist you work in fundraising promotions only, rather than across the board of marketing. Or as a computer consultant who worked in database systems before, now you specialize in FoxPro systems. Or you are a security specialist who now restricts your practice to alarm systems only. Now you can really focus your efforts.

But wait a minute. As an independent consultant you are in business. Let's ponder this: There are certain critical functions in a business, any business, whether it is a giant corporation with a vast chain of outlets or a peddler selling shoelaces. To conduct any business, you must first have something to sell. You have that already: You are going to sell your expert services to help your clients solve their problems.

Of course, you must also have clients. Having something to sell doesn't help you much until you find people to sell it to. It's called *sales* or *marketing*. (They are not really the same thing, strictly speaking, but let's let that go for now.)

You will have to have certain assets necessary to your business, but we will assume that you have no need for major investment capital, as discussed earlier.

You need to keep records. One reason is because the IRS will get pretty unhappy with you if you can't document your income and expenses, and they can make you pretty unhappy too. But fear of the IRS is not the sole reason and should not be even the main reason for good recordkeeping. *You* also need the information that only well-kept, accurate accounting records can provide, and they can make the difference between success and failure.

These are the three most basic, most critically essential items in any business, especially those first two—something to sell and someone to sell it to. And since you are a one-person enterprise, you have a few things to do, other than consulting, to keep your business going. Who is going to do all these other things—keep the books, make the sales, answer the telephone, write bids and quotations, order supplies, get reports typed and printed, and all the other annoyingly necessary chores—to keep the business running? Yes, it's you, of course. Who else is there?

You can be the specialist part of the time, but only part of the time. The rest of the time you have to be the generalist—accountant, purchasing agent, typist, marketer, writer, and general administrator.

Can you do all of this, managing all the daily problems, and still have time to practice your specialty? Yes, you probably can, if you don't mind working eighteen hours a day. Or you can prepare a solid, well thought out business plan that will cover much of this and leave you more time to be the specialist and some time for yourself as an individual. Among other things, it will point out where and how to get outside help—an accountant, for example—that will not only relieve you of some of the pressures but will probably get the job done better and probably at lesser real cost.

That is essentially what we are talking about here: the business plan as a road map for some, who need a charted path to follow, and a lifeline for others, who would be in danger of drowning in a sea of "other work" and daily problems. The business plan is not a luxury; it is a necessity, if you want to enjoy long-term success, rather than to settle for daily survival.

Probably everyone who starts any enterprise believes that he or she has a plan. That word, "plan," is a rather flexible term, and I am sure that the plan you and most other consultants conceived was one thought out mentally as a set of resolutions but never committed to paper in organized form. Probably you reasoned, as the future consultant, even if you did not articulate it in a set of words: "I am going to now sell my services as a consultant, at some rate I will determine later. I will set up an office at home, put an ad in the papers, mail out a few brochures, and have some business cards printed up, after which I shall be independent, secure, and live happily ever after."

I suppose you can call that a plan, even call it a business plan. Perhaps I did that, too; I can't recall now, although I do recall false starts and starting over a few times. After all, you have the technical skills, you have worked in the industry, you know quite a few people in it, you can probably make a few telephone calls to get your first contracts. You might even get some work from your former employer. What more would you need?

A Course Correction

There is the unfortunate habit we all fall into of referring to this process as *writing* a business plan, as though it were an exercise in writing well—that is, as though writing skills would translate into business plan excellence. It is analogous to the situation vis-à-vis developing proposals, where constant reference to *writing* a proposal, rather than *developing* and *building* it, leads often to losing sight of what it is and needs to be, which is a sales presentation, of course.

Here, the opposite is the case: If you are writing your business plan as a tool to pursue financing, the plan would, indeed, be a sales presentation. If you have partners or business associates you must persuade to accept your assessment and plan, that would also make your plan a sales presentation. But we already have decided as our premises that you will not need outside financing and you are an independent operator. Your business plan is thus anything but a sales presentation. It is a road map, as accurate as you can make it at the moment. It should be as close to blunt and even brutal truth as possible. It is preparation for meeting and solving the myriad of problems you must solve to launch and run a successful consulting practice.

Of course, literally, you will write your business plan, but the writing itself, skillful or not, is relatively unimportant, and we must not lose sight of this truth. A more appropriate phrase would be "business plan development," to remind ourselves that creating a business plan is a *process*, a long and laborious one, if it is to produce a worthy product, one that does the job.

A Second Course Correction: Expect to Change Your Plan

While there is reason to think of a business plan in terms of detailed plans and preparations for a start-up, it is most often a plan with the details only penciled in. That is, it is a plan subject to expected review and revision, as it should be. It is a firm plan but it is not chiseled into stone because it is largely estimates—call them "guesstimates" as many do—and it should be reviewed as often as possible, to be revised as circumstances dictate. Often, the original business plan should be scrapped and a new one drawn up, accommodating the inevitable changes that take place in the course of conducting a business and making corrections to refine rough estimates made earlier. (After the dust has settled, and the practice seems to be reasonably well established, you may review your plan as infrequently as annually, but in the first year or two, the reviews should be frequent, almost continuous, as experience validates, invalidates, and modifies early projections.)

Elizabeth M. Jay, proprietor of Papyrus & Silicon Inc. of New York City, provides proofreading and copyediting services to businesses nationwide, mainly via fax and modem, although she also sends staff people to provide her services on-site to clients in the city. Commenting on business plans, she says:

> I wrote a formal business plan prior to starting my company. About six months later, the business plan was almost entirely revised because my ideas had changed. Now I update my business plan once or twice a year, and even if there aren't a lot of revisions, it helps just to reread the thing.
>
> I make lists constantly. The lists are usually very short-term. They're constantly revised as I either finish items, decide I don't

care about certain things anyway, and add new items. I wouldn't
be able to get anything done without them. I have one list that's
for daily and weekly things and another that's for larger projects
that don't have strict deadlines. Stuff like reorganizing files
comes under the latter.

Bear always in mind that while every business venture ought to be
based on a business plan, the enormous variability in business ventures mandates an almost equally enormous variability in the plans.
Many of the features are common to all, of course, but many are—
must be—peculiar to the industry or business and to the individual
circumstances surrounding the establishment and conduct of the
business. Jane Smith and Pete Jones may be in nominally identical
ventures, but there will still be many individual differences, and
these must be reflected in the two business plans. Even then, as Elizabeth Jay notes, it is necessary to revise the plan periodically, especially in the early years of a new enterprise, when you are feeling your
way and adjusting your operations to the realities you encounter.
Consciously or unconsciously, your ideas change. As a result, it is rare
that one winds up doing what he or she expected to be doing in
business, as in life.

For example, Charles Aronson, of Arcade, New York, started out
to establish a custom machine shop. Circumstances, largely in the
nature of cutthroat competitors, forced him to become a machine
"job shop" for a time, but in the end he became a leading—perhaps
the leading—manufacturer of welding positioners, a rather specialized kind of machine. Similarly, Milton Hershey did not set out to
create the world's best known chocolate. He had manufactured cara-
mel and other candies first and had more than one business failure.
Elisha Otis also had several business failures before establishing his
elevator manufacturing company, so well known today. It's easy
enough to find these stories because they are typical, and they match
your story and mine. Even if reality matched our plans and expecta-
tions, as it so rarely does, chance takes a hand in our lives and in our
business ventures, and we also simply change our minds when we
find an experience disappointing. Your business plan is of reduced

value, and possibly of no value, to you unless you revise it to match your new ideas and goals.

Expect it. Plan to update and revise your plan—not once or twice, but many times. Keep it up to date, as you keep your checkbook stubs and your ledgers up to date. It's just as important.

HOW BIG SHOULD A BUSINESS PLAN BE?

As part of my research, I reviewed a business plan offered by Price-Waterhouse as an example. It was a plan for a high-technology manufacturing company, and was thirty-eight pages long. The executive summary alone was more than three pages. It described the company's products and extolled their virtues, outlined the financing the company was seeking, projected the good news of the company's promising future in a market described in optimistic terms, painted a picture of fine management, and presented flattering thumbnail sketches of its founders and operating officials.

That is not atypical for the average business plan, but as a one-person enterprise you won't need anything quite that elaborate. Since you are not asking anyone for money, you have no need to gild the lily. You can and should be painfully honest, even blunt, in presenting the stark facts; there isn't much point in lying to yourself or covering up facts. Since you are writing it for yourself primarily (although it will be most helpful in explaining your business to an accountant, lawyer, advertising executive, or other specialist you may wish to consult from time to time), it is really not necessary to describe to yourself your professional qualifications and other such items. They would be useful in reassuring an investor or lender of your worthiness as an investment or loan risk but they can serve no useful purpose otherwise. Consider the hypothetical executive summary on the next page as an example for an independent consulting practice.

The sample summary is written for an existing enterprise but could easily have been written in future tense to describe an enter-

Executive Summary

HRH Communications Inc. is a consulting business that provides marketing support and training, especially in proposal writing, for contractors to the federal government. It earns revenue and profit by billing at a daily rate for direct support in writing proposals and related services, both on- and off-site, and by conducting on-site custom training seminars for clients. It is operated as a shareholder-owned company. It began in 1974 and was founded by Herman Holtz. HRH Communications Inc. currently has 2 employees and is profitable.

We sell our services in a national market. There are approximately 250,000 firms doing business regularly with the government. Among the approximately 15 million other firms are many more who could win government business if they were motivated to do so. They represent major growth potential for the business.

We believe we enjoy about 2% of the market and could capture 5% of the market. What we sell to our clients is the skill and knowledge that produced more than $360 million in government contracts for former employers and clients directly, and has trained hundreds of proposal writers for many firms. We have the capacity to bring firms who have never done business with the government into the circle of government contractors, and we should address that potential market.

We market principally by the indirect means of PR activities, including active membership in associations, public speaking, our own (free) newsletter, press releases, and various writings in journals and magazines.

We have an advantage over competitors in that our services are far more specialized than theirs because we aid the client in designing the program to be offered, as well as writing an outstanding proposal, based on the technical, cost, and presentation strategies we devise for clients. We use and make available to clients many techniques that are trade secrets of HRH Communications, such as how to appear to be the low bidder in laundry list contracts, how to find worry items and how to handle requests for proposals that do not reveal such items, how to respond to vague requirements, how to take exceptions while avoiding nonresponsiveness, and many other tactics and strategies.

Our overhead rate is 67%, with a 3% general and administrative burden, and we subcontract to associates when we find ourselves overloaded, or use temporary services for administrative work, rather than hiring permanent employees.

prise about to be launched. It does not include budgetary and related data, except for specifying overhead and other burden rates.
Even these are summarized most briefly as only a reminder to you of
some broad objectives, what you sell, and what your general strategy
is. The only others who will read it, ordinarily, will be those from
whom you seek advice or guidance of some sort. For your purposes, it
is rarely necessary or useful to prepare a financial statement of more
than a page or two and a business plan of more than a few pages.

2

Mission Statements and Business Definitions

Do you know what business you are in or plan to be in? Do you have a truly clear view of the mission of your practice or contemplated practice? It can be surprisingly difficult to find a useful definition, even when you think you know exactly what it is you plan to do. You may have to arrive at more than one definition, even for what you think is a simple and straightforward business idea. Keep your mind open: You may be in for a surprise or two.

MAKING A START

In the introduction of this book, the first item in the bobtailed business plan outline was the mission statement. Ideally, a mission statement defines the business. One mission statement I read recently stated that the company was in the business of serving the needs of hospitals and businesses serving home care needs. The statement was not only vague and general, it was inaccurate. In fact, the company was organized to *develop new products* for use in hospitals and for home care of patients. That is not the same thing at all as was said in the mission statement, and was not stated or even implied in defining or describing the business. Were the framers of that business plan truly confused about precisely what they planned to do and the basic strategy of their business concept? It is quite possible that they had not thought things through and did not realize that "serving the needs" was vague and conveyed almost nothing to a reader, whereas "developing new products" would be far more specific and represented at least the suggestion of why that business should be launched and how it was conceived as having something upon which to base its plans for success. However, the real damage is done in a case such as this when the business owners do not have a clear idea of what they plan to do for customers. How do you sell whatever it is you have to sell when you don't have a clear idea of what you are selling?

The First Draft

Thinking things through and choosing the right words, words that say something, is a beginning. But it is only a beginning. There is a great deal more to think about and discuss before you are ready to write your mission statement in final form. Make no mistake, writing a mission statement is important to your success. It tells you where you are going or, at least, where you intended to go when you started. And if you have not decided where you intend to go, don't be surprised if you wind up at the wrong place! That is why you should try writing a first-draft mission statement now. You'll revise it later, after I cover a few more things about it, but it will help if you make an effort to do it now.

The objective is to compel you to think about your business with some degree of logic and precision. If you do not have a clear image of what your venture is or ought to be, this is an excellent time to discover that shortcoming of vision and the need for overcoming it. You may find it difficult to think things out at first; a great many people do. They take comfort in saying, "I know what it is, but I don't know how to say it." The simple truth is that if you don't know how to say it—how to put the idea into words—you probably are dealing only in vague notions and don't really know what your mission is, except in some rambling way. You are strolling idly along, without a clear goal or plan, hoping that something will happen along the way to give you direction. Of course, you don't believe this now and perhaps don't understand the need to even think about it now. Later, when you have finally gotten a clear and direct mission statement drawn up, you will understand this much better.

I suggest that you do this mission statement in three phases: Stop here and do the first one now, without further preparation or instruction. It need only be a sentence or two, but it should be spontaneous, what you think at this moment is a proper statement of the mission of your practice. It is important that you do this now and be able to refer to it later, when you are in the second and third phases. When you have done so, read on, and revise your mission statement accordingly. You will probably make drastic changes. As you read further in this chapter and closely examine the definition of your business, I think you will be ready to revise your mission statement and put it into final form.

Help for a Second Draft

With your initial draft completed, go on to read through the next portion of this chapter, which offers you a bit of help, preparatory to revising your draft statement. Think about your ideas, whether you are still contemplating a start or have been in practice for a while. The latter circumstance does not obviate the need to think about what your business is. Many people are in business for years, plodding along and placidly going nowhere because they never planned to go anywhere. A large element of your mission statement is to at least suggest, if not to precisely define, where you wish to go and how you plan to get there—that is, why people should and will become your clients.

Think in concrete words—verbs and nouns. Shun all adjectives and adverbs: They lead to superlatives and other hyperbole, which do nothing except obscure the facts and encourage you to think

---

List of Teaser Items

Answer every question, and rank in order of importance those choices given in the second question. Think hard about why you are in business—your primary motive, especially—and what you hope to accomplish over time:

- What kind of consulting services do you provide?
- Why are you in business?

    □ Money
    □ Love the work
    □ Independence and freedom
    □ Love the lifestyle
    □ Other

- What needs or wants do you satisfy?
- Whose needs or wants do you satisfy?
- Are your clients the consumers or intermediates?
- How is your service different/better than that of competitors?

---

wishfully. Write a draft and then review it mercilessly to scratch out such vague and general terms as "serve" and "respond."

See the teaser items in the box. They should stimulate and channel your thinking a bit. Consider the questions and think hard about your answers: Within those answers lie keys to the information you need to begin developing. Then you should be able to revise your first draft and address your mission more clearly. The questions are intended to guide you in determining what you are really about in your venture, for they are important questions. It will help shake the cobwebs out if you spend the time to think about each of the items and be perfectly honest with yourself. Your answers are for your eyes only, so you can afford to be honest about them. Go on, once you have the answers you worked out, to write a second mission statement as a revision of your original draft.

WHAT BUSINESS ARE YOU IN?

An observation about business and management that struck me and has stayed firmly in the forefront of my thinking was one made by Peter Drucker many years ago in one of his books, *The Practice of Management* (Harper & Row, 1956). In that book Drucker reported discovering that many business owners he encountered did not know what business they were in, and he postulated this as a common problem, without discussing it directly. It gave me trouble for a long time, as I pondered the meaning of this observation. I was sure that Drucker had not said this idly; it had to be a significant point, and yet I was not sure just what he had meant. How could anyone not know what their business was? Did a steel manufacturer not know that his business was making and selling steel? A dairy farmer not know that he produced and sold milk? A computer consultant not know that he sold computer services, his expert knowledge about computers?

In conducting research for this book, I reviewed many books, articles, and sophisticated computer programs that offered extended discussions of business plans, instructions for writing them, suggested outlines, and sample programs. Some of those were hypothetical, some were actual plans that had been written by or for existing and planned businesses, and some offered actual computer templates of various kinds from which business plans could be modeled. Plans, templates, guidelines, and outlines varied widely, but there were certain areas of nearly complete agreement. One of them was a clear requirement to identify or describe the business.

Dr. Joseph R. Mancuso, founder and director of The Center for Entrepreneurial Management Inc. and author of many books, must have been struck very much as I was by Drucker's observation, for he also raises the need to answer the question "What business am I in?" and cites Drucker for raising the issue of defining one's business in his (Mancuso's) own book, *How to Write a Winning Business Plan* (Prentice-Hall, 1985). He notes the importance of answering the question accurately, but freely confesses that it is not an easy task in any given case, and with that I can concur. Despite the difficulty, however, I believe it is a question that must be answered in a suitable context or frame of reference, which means that there is no single answer, no formula, no template for it. It is a question that has more than one answer. I believe that to answer the question effectively, you must consider *why* and *for whom* you are answering the question. Therein lies its special importance and special significance here. If anyone wishes to know what business you are in and asks you the question, you must first respond (at least silently, to yourself), "Who wants to know?"

Who Wants to Know?

"Who wants to know?" is significant because the answer to the question, "What business are you in?" has real meaning only in context of one's own perception, which is, of course, influenced greatly by individual interests. The supplier trying to sell you something has an entirely different interest and perception than the prospective client to whom you hope to sell your services, and who wants to know what your business is only in terms of that interest. Each vendor is in search of a definition that provides a clue as to what you may be a prospective client for, while the prospective client wants to know what you have to offer that may be of interest to him or her. You don't care a great deal about what potential vendors perceive, unless you are looking to them for expert advice. You are interested in what clients and, especially, prospective clients perceive. Their perceptions define your business.

You Don't Always Arrive at Your Original Destination

A great many businesses evolve into something quite different than they started out to be, usually as a result of how customers respond and react. Customer demand or acceptance causes an accounting or engineering firm to evolve into a consulting firm, as it caused a securities broker to evolve into a newsletter publisher, and a beer and wine shop into a luncheonette. Your business is what your clients decide it is. A small, home-based mail order dealer I knew tried selling a variety of items, but his customers decided he was a printing broker, especially of business cards, and soon that was his main business. He succeeded because he did not fight his customers' wishes, but began to acquire sample books and connections to fulfill a wide variety of desires in business cards. An author of a number of books of his own was perceived by others as a ghostwriter, writing others' books for them, and soon that was his main writing effort. The Hoover vacuum cleaner company was originally in the leather harness business. The well-known electronic-parts supplier, P. J. Mallory, started out to manufacture tungsten filaments for the then new electric light bulb. John Deere, who makes a variety of farm tools, was a blacksmith when he invented a new kind of plow to solve a special problem local farmers were having.

Ask Your Clients What Business You Are In

The most effective way—and possibly the only effective way—to define your business is by gauging how your customers perceive you. I have a computer guru I rely on. He has built and maintained my computers for me for nearly ten years. He thought of himself as a computer manufacturer. To me, he has always been a white knight, a rescuer: When I have computer disasters that are beyond my skills to master, I call him and he rescues me unfailingly, sometimes even with directions over the telephone. I never ask his price. I know he will be reasonable, and I would pay what he asked in any case. That is, of course, a highly desirable image to earn, but its value to you depends on your understanding that you have that image and then turning it to your advantage.

The Classic Case

The classic case that best illustrates the problem of defining your business is that of the railroads, whose managers insisted stubbornly that they were in the "railroad" business, even as airplanes, buses, trucks, and huge tractor-trailers were taking over the business, and the railroads were rapidly dying. The experts with 20/20 hindsight will tell you today that the railroads were in the transportation business, and the moguls who owned and ran the railroads ought to have known it. They should have known that airlines, bus companies, and private automobiles were taking away almost all of their passenger business, and the truck lines were taking over much of the freight business. But the railroad owners insisted the word "railroad" was self-defining, that any fool knew railroads were in the transportation business.

That may be so. Maybe they were in the transportation business, but saying so wasn't good enough. Nor would changing their definition from "railroads" to "transportation" have solved the problem for them. They had to begin to *think* transportation, and base their actions and decisions on it so they could compete effectively, as far as moving freight for customers was concerned. They had to think what kinds of needs railroads served best, what kinds of prospective customers had such needs, and how those customers could be persuaded to perceive the railroad as the best way to satisfy that need.

Thinking that way would have told them that they were in two businesses, not one: Freight transportation is one business, but transporting people is not the transportation business; it is the travel business, quite another business and another industry.

Why, for example, would an individual needing to travel to another place choose the railroad over an airline or bus line? Air travel is faster, but it requires traveling to and from an inconveniently located airport. It's expensive. It's a bit uncomfortable, at least in the coach section and especially when the flight is full. And, in many people's perceptions, it is hazardous. Bus travel, on the other hand, is slow and no more comfortable than crowded airplanes.

The railroad is a good compromise between the two for speed, and much more comfortable than either airplanes or buses. You also get to see some of the countryside, something you see little of from an airplane. And you can leave from within the city and arrive within the city, a major convenience. Even now, railroads do not do much of a job of selling this to prospective passengers. Their business is, or ought to be, getting you there safely, comfortably, and conveniently, and avoiding the problems of travel to and from airports at both ends of the flight.

Transporting freight by railroad is an entirely different matter. Probably the largest advantage is cost. Railroads can move large quantities of freight at less cost than trucking lines, generally. But the railroaders did catch on belatedly to other possibilities of working with trucking companies by piggybacking trailers on flatcars between cities, to everybody's greater profit. Their business could be defined to shippers as getting your freight there at lowest cost.

There is a parallel in the entertainment world. There was, originally, only one kind of customer for Hollywood movies: the theater owners. As the movie industry developed, theaters sprang up all over the country. And then TV appeared.

The Hollywood movie moguls fought TV in every way they could, including forbidding their own contract actors to appear on TV, and even blackballing or threatening to blackball actors who appeared on TV. Eventually, they discovered that TV was the best thing that ever happened to Hollywood, as TV became a major consumer of movies, and the salvation of many bad movies that lost money in the theaters. The videocassette recorder has resulted in closing a major portion of the country's public movie theaters, but sales of movies in cassettes have been a huge boon to movie makers. Movies on the small screen (TV) have become today's principal home entertainment, and that is the definition by which most consumers see that industry. But TV executives see it as a major source of material to fill their programming hours. Again, different definitions for different customers.

Another Example

This kind of analysis works for consultants, too, in helping us get a better handle on our business and our markets. Thus "I am a security consultant" may provide a clue to all who are interested, but it doesn't say enough. "What kind of security?" most will want to know.

To some, security may mean locks, safes, and alarms safeguarding property and possessions. To others, it may mean surveillance and armed guards. It may mean protecting their computer systems from viruses and break-ins, or even employee and prospective employee investigations, such as are routine in certain industries, especially where employees are bonded. And it may mean, especially to wealthy individuals and to celebrated public figures, personal protection from potential kidnappers, assassins, stalkers, and even rabid fans and groupies. People who are private investigators sometimes take on tasks such as these, although many make it their main activity to conduct personal background checks on employees and prospective employees, another form of security services. Thus, you think of yourself as a private investigator but your client sees you as a security specialist.

Even if you define yourself by the broad term "security consultant" or in some narrower term, such as "computer security consultant," what you have done is to define your business from *your* viewpoint, whereas clients, suppliers, bankers, investors, and other parties want a definition from their viewpoints. Theirs are strongly influenced by the clients' needs and wants, of course. They look at your business for what it will do for them. Consider a few alternatives:

- I inspect and analyze my clients' operations and prepare complete security plans.
- I plug the holes in a security system to safeguard my client's trade secrets.
- I burglar-proof my clients' premises physically with all necessary locks and alarms.
- I burglar-proof my client's data and communications systems.
- I enable my clients to avoid hiring people who are security risks.

Even these are only the beginnings of definitions, but they do begin to explain what you mean by security. Let's go a step further: "I develop complete security systems, implement them, and do periodic checks on them for my clients, to safeguard their facilities physically against break-ins and to prevent leaks of their trade secrets."

That is the beginning of a definition that imparts some specific information to prospective clients and to others. It is a premise that you are not writing a loan proposal, and I will assume that you are not going to make efforts to make life easier for suppliers. That leaves prospective clients as the people for whom you will need to define your business. But wait—there is one other party who needs to understand what business you are in as much as anyone does: *you.* In writing a business plan, it is you who wants to know.

What Do You *Do?*

The point is, of course, that your definition of your business ought to be in the client's terms or from the client's viewpoint: It ought to specify what you *do* for your clients. Does your client really want to spend a great deal of money for locks, safes, guards, inspections, alarms, and other such measures? Of course not; your client wants security. Locks, safes, inspections, guards, alarms are not *what* you do or *why* you do them; they are only *how* you do what you do. *Security* is what you do. Be sure you understand the difference: Clients don't really care about how, except as they need some kind of logical proof that you can and do deliver what you promise. Ergo, promise security, not locks and alarms. You are not in the lock, safe, guard, or alarm business; you are in the security business. However, the mere word "security" does not convey the message, any more than the word "transportation" really defined the railroad business.

I consulted for a few years as a proposal writer. That was and is an unfortunate term. A prospective client asks me what I do, and I say, "I write proposals." Whether it is proposals I write or something else doesn't matter; I am immediately identified in the prospect's mind as a writer: This fellow is a writer. If I needed a writer, I might call on him. But I don't need a writer; I need business—contracts. I need a "contract getter."

Yes, that business description as a proposal writing business certainly not only identifies me and my business, but it also suggests that the principal skill needed to turn out a good proposal is writing skill. If true, any good writer ought to be a good proposal writer. So the average prospect would reason, understandably enough.

Suppose that instead of labeling myself as a writer of proposals, when asked what I do, I say, "I help people win contracts." I rather suspect that such a description of what I do would strike a nerve with most people in business. It's a rather short answer, but it has the elements of a sales presentation: It is brief, in simple language, and easy to grasp immediately. Most important, it makes the direct promise of a benefit. All this in only five words!

The truth about proposal writing is that while some writing skill is needed, that is probably the least important of the several skills required to produce outstanding proposals. The first and most important skill is marketing, and that means a great deal more than a mere knowledge of the principles of sales and marketing. It includes that understanding but also a talent for sales and marketing, because it requires at least as much art as method to do it well. It calls for the talent for conceiving and implementing strategies. And it calls for a sense of and skill in producing an effective presentation. My consulting business was not proposal writing; it was winning contracts. That is what clients paid me to do for them. Writing proposals was merely *how* I did what I did for them—helping them win contracts.

There is a great deal to explain about the art of writing proposals that win contracts—and, of course, those are the only proposals worth writing—but first I need to get the prospect's attention, and those five words are quite likely to do just that. It seems quite obvious now, but it took me some time to learn that "I help people win contracts" is a tremendously different statement than "I write proposals."

Not all my clients hired me to help them win specific contracts, however. Many hired me to teach their staffs how to win contracts. They had me conduct in-house seminars in proposal writing for their staffs. But while I was teaching proposal writing, teaching writing per se was not my business. My business was showing their staffs how to win contracts. My business was teaching them how to appear to be the low bidder, even when they were not. My business was teaching them how to avoid ever having problems collecting their bills from government agencies. My business was teaching them how to prevent contract disputes and conflicts. My business was teaching them dozens of such tips and techniques.

On one occasion, a prospective client rebelled at my rate. She insisted that I was far too high priced for a mere writer. I tried to explain that the act of writing the proposal was the least of what I did, that I was a consultant with a great many more important skills and knowledge than that of writing. It did no good. No matter what I said, my prospective client insisted that I was only a writer and not worth a consultant's fee. This tale is significant for two reasons: It illustrates the down side of an improper definition of your business—of who and what you are. It also happens to be the only time I ran into this problem over all the years I provided my services to help clients win contracts and train their staffs in winning contracts, and I believe that illustrates the up side of having been at pains always to explain what I did in terms of what it meant to clients.

Client's Needs or Wants Define Your Businesses

Most of us are in more than one business, in the sense of being in a business that satisfies the needs of our clients, even if we practice a narrow specialty. Let us suppose that you are a direct marketing consultant and the service you perform, from your viewpoint, is that of designing and creating direct mail packages. The typical assignment you undertake is to counsel your clients and write some or all of their materials—salesletters, brochures, order forms, broadsides, lift letters, and similar materials. You offer to do any or all design and creative work on the packages because your clients are in various businesses and so view their needs and problems differently. One client is a magazine publisher, the next one is a promoter of one item at a time, and the next one sells men's apparel.

You may say that you are a direct marketing consultant serving all these clients in that capacity. But how do the clients see you and what you do for them?

The magazine publisher is in the advertising business, if he or she has defined the business well: The profitability of a magazine depends on the publisher's success in selling advertising. That publisher may see you as the key to winning greater sales of advertising space. The promoter selling one item at a time usually needs a sharply focused, intense promotion, especially if the item is a fad item, and sees you in terms of increasing direct sales. The seller of men's apparel is probably focused on creating customers, rather than immediate sales, as the key to his or her success. You are thus looked to as a winner of customers. Each of these clients wants to see you as a specialist in his or her own field, not in some general field. They tend to have great difficulty in seeing anyone as equally effective in two or more fields.

But wait: Most clients' needs change also. That magazine publisher also needs circulation—subscribers and newsstand purchasers (with subscribers by far the more desirable kind of reader to win)—in order to be an attractive advertising medium and to command good advertising rates. And so while you might be the specialist in attracting advertisers, you must also be the specialist in attracting subscribers.

But even that is not the end. One of the keys to periodical success is a high renewal rate, and so most publishers of periodicals make many kinds of offers to urge subscribers to renew their subscriptions. Here, again, your business is the same, and yet it is different.

In short, then, while you may think that what you do for all clients and in all cases is the same thing, what clients want is not the same thing. Even a given client does not always want the same service as the last time you were retained by that client. One assignment calls primarily for counseling: The client wants your advice on general marketing strategy. The next assignment is with a client who wants to benefit from your services as a master salesletter writer.

Is all of this nit-picking? Mere semantics? Does it really matter? Yes, it matters a great deal. It matters in understanding your clients, how they think, what motivates them, and how to appeal to them. It matters in how well you understand your business—what you are selling. It matters in thinking out what you want to accomplish and how you must go about it—essential ingredients that are at the heart of your business plan.

You Are in More Than One Business

By now it may have occurred to you that it is not only not easy to define your business, but you are probably—almost surely, in fact—in more than one business. Do your clients understand that? Here is one example of what clients do and do not understand.

I once managed a substantially large group of publications experts, writing technical manuals on contract. We had won a contract with a local firm to write manuals for them. One day I learned, purely by chance, that this client was soliciting proposals for a contract to do illustrating work for them. I confronted the manager of that company and asked why we were not invited to compete for that contract, in light of our current friendly and satisfactory working relationships.

He was taken aback, completely surprised.

"Do you do illustrating too?" he asked.

It had not occurred to him that any large publications group, especially one writing technical manuals, would necessarily have a staff of artists to illustrate their manuals. He thought of illustrating as another business, not related to writing!

Such misconceptions are not at all unusual. Your clients will inevitably and unfailingly mentally tag you as some narrowly defined specialist and probably have a poor understanding of everything you do, no matter what you call your company or what your business card or brochure says. You must work at making them aware of *all* the services you have to offer, and even then most will not get the message. That is what is wrong with having a single, general brochure, even a single business card; you need a different one for *each* of the businesses you are in, for each of the services you offer. I helped clients write proposals; I helped them train their staffs in writing proposals; I helped them solve proposal-related problems, such as analyzing the request for proposals (RFP) and devising strategies; I helped them organize their proposal teams. I was a counselor; I was a proposal writer; I was a strategist; I was a presentation specialist—all in response to whatever the client's need or problem was.

How many different businesses is that? Several, at least, for this reason: The client who wants only a couple of hours of my time to help analyze an RFP and formulate a response strategy may fear calling me because of an assumption that I don't do less than all-out support. (Clients are human, and they do the same leaping to mistaken conclusions and operating on inaccurate assumptions that you and I do.) I must somehow make the client aware that it is possible to retain me for lesser help than full support. But first I must make myself aware of it—aware, that is, in that I must understand the client's needs and problems.

It is in my efforts to understand those needs and problems that at the earliest possible time in any discussion with a prospective client (even those who are not yet even suspects, much less prospects) I begin to ask questions, probing to learn those things. I need the other's help in finding out what business I am in at the moment, for my business is always solving the problems and satisfying the needs of my client.

DEVELOPING YOUR BUSINESS DEFINITIONS

Even though it's true that consultants engage in "different" businesses, you cannot be in a different business every day or several times a day. There has to be some stability to your businesses. That means, in the practical terms of the needs of your business plan, you must develop a reasonable number of definitions, targeted closely to support an efficient marketing plan but constrained enough to be feasible. Whether you realize it or not, your business definition is, in each case, the consequence of a client's needs and problems. Thus, what you must do as a first step is to decide who and what your clients are to develop a reasonable number of client profiles. You must identify your clients. Make an analysis by answering the questions in the box on the facing page. You should logically start by compiling a fairly large list in responding to the first item, and reduce the list steadily as you proceed through the remaining items. By the time you reach the last item, you should have a manageable number, probably three to five. They should also be segregated in such a manner that the distinctions among them are clear-cut and do represent somewhat different interests.

The Chicken and the Egg

You may or may not have noticed immediately that this is a kind of chicken-and-egg problem: To find out what your clients' problems are, you must decide who they are. But how can you decide who they

---

Who Are the Best Prospects for Your Services?

1. Decide who are the natural prospects for what you do. What kinds of clients—clients in what businesses or professions—are most likely to need or greatly benefit from what you do?
2. Which of these are numerous enough—constitute a large enough niche—to be worth pursuing?
3. Which of these are you most able to reach with your marketing efforts?
4. Which of these are most likely to retain you as an independent consultant and contractor?

---

are without making assumptions about their needs? Thus, carrying out these steps must be an iterative process accomplished through a series of approximations. That high-blown phrase means, simply put, that first you must make some general assumptions of who your prospective clients are, then judge their needs in general, then return to the first step and narrow the definition somewhat, and continue this process until you are satisfied that you have identified your businesses and your best prospects. For example, if you are a computer consultant, everyone in almost any business is a potential client, but you must narrow that immediately within the implications of your own specialty—that is, if your specialty is inventory management and control software, you know that only businesses that maintain substantial inventories are prospects logically.

What Are Your Prospects' Typical Needs and Problems?

Having made the general observation that you must seek out prospects who maintain large inventories, you must begin to subdivide and classify those prospects to identify their problems and match the problems with the services you can or wish to offer. Here, for example, are only a few possible classes and categories of prospects carrying large inventories:

- Inventories with a great number of items.
- Inventories of complex and interrelated items.
- Inventories of large items requiring extensive storage facilities.
- Inventories subject to hazards of pilferage and burglary.
- Wholesale inventories.
- Retail inventories.
- Inventories containing both short- and long-lead items.

Any organization supplying automotive parts is likely to fit several of these categories. One serving the construction industry would require large storage facilities, much of it outdoors. Inventories of consumer goods would be subject to hazards of pilfering and burglary.

The next step would be to decide which of these problems your services can best address. Thus your businesses might be the maintenance of timely ordering of items to ensure proper service to the client's customers, the instant detection of unexplained depletions in inventory (detection of losses), the minimizing of losses through item obsolescence, and the relief for still other problems of inventory management and control. The U.S. Postal Service, for example, operates some 300 "vehicle maintenance centers"—garages—and has always had the problem of storing millions of dollars worth of parts, many of them for older vehicles, so obsolescence is a problem.

Estimates of needs at this step is based on the assumption that you are still in the planning stages. If you are already established in your practice, you are going to base these analyses and estimates on your actual experience and knowledge of the industry(ies) you serve. This study will probably open you up to some new ideas, and expand your field of operations.

Be Prepared to Implement Your Plan

One executive who wrote business plans for project managers in his company reports a special problem that few business-plan writers have mentioned. He found that quite often those for whom he wrote business plans did not take appropriate follow-up action to implement the plans. He did not at first understand this. In time, when he left salaried employment and launched his own business, he came to a sudden understanding of the problem: Many of the steps required to carry out the plan—even to define one's business—require initiative and courage to implement, especially in the established business, where implementation probably means change. The reluctance to accept change is a common problem.

Implementation imposes a requirement for firm commitment, and while there is certainly nothing wrong in getting professional help to write your business plan, you must be sure that you participate actively in the process if you have hired a business-plan specialist. You must be fully conscious of the decisions you make, and be prepared to accept them and implement the plan. Therefore, think carefully about what the various provisions in the plan are going to require in the way of implementation before you commit yourself to those provisions. Make the plan what you want it to be, a plan you will be willing to carry out completely and without delay. Agreed that the plan is not chiseled in stone, and you should review it and modify it, as necessary, but that is not a license to procrastinate putting the plan to work. The changes should come about from experience with the plan, and not from faintheartedness in execution.

THE FINAL MISSION STATEMENT

Now that you have a much better understanding of what your business is, you should be ready to write a final mission statement. It should be expressed in nouns and verbs with few adjectives or adverbs and no superlatives. It should suggest, as clearly as you can manage in a sentence or two, these things:

- What you do for clients, as clients are likely to view what you do for them—that is, the benefit they derive.
- The basis of your appeal—your business strategy: to whom you plan to address your appeals for their patronage and what makes your offering superior and more appealing to clients.
- Your long-range view and goal.

Try working at it until you are satisfied that you have accomplished this description as well as it can be accomplished in this first business plan. Consider it a final draft, but it is possible that by the time you have completed your business plan you will have other ideas and wish to change your mission statement yet again. You may even want to change it after you have drafted the rest of your business plan and have gained greater insights into what you will be doing—when you write an executive summary, that is.

ONE MISSION STATEMENT OR SEVERAL?

It is clear that you are probably going to be in more than one business, even if you never develop ancillary income activities. Unless there is some remarkable uniformity among your clients, different groups or subsets of your client population will have different needs and will therefore employ you somewhat differently. That means, too, that they must view you somewhat differently. The client who calls on you to provide services he does not know how to provide or lacks the capability to provide for himself sees you as an expert to turn to when his needs are unusual or he is in serious trouble, much as I look to my computer guru as my rescuer—my hero—when I am in computer trouble. The client who calls on you when she is overloaded and her staff can't keep up sees you as ancillary staff. The client who calls on you to conduct seminars for his staff sees you as a training consultant, and so on.

You can write a complex mission statement several paragraphs or even several pages long to cover all of these viewpoints, but that is self-defeating. The idea of writing a mission statement is to sum up the mission briefly and without the confusion of excess verbiage. It is far better to view each major variant in your services—that is, a major variant in the nature of the clients served—as a separate mission that merits its own mission statement. Thus you may have more than one mission statement, and should have no hesitancy about having several such statements, each one geared to the services you provide some group of clients. If you add services—seminars, newsletters, or routine maintenance, for example—you will want to add mission statements to cover these. Some sample mission statements follow, including a few to show multiple mission statements of the same consultancy.

Sample Mission Statements

Jason & Associates, copy specialists, will provide to small businesses in Williams County complete design, copywriting, and art services for all print media on a quick-response basis.

Jason & Associates, copy specialists, will provide to all selling by direct mail in Williams County complete design, writing, and production services for direct-mail campaigns in a quick-response service.

Peter Murdock, consulting engineer, will provide electronic chip design services in digital applications to all clients on a national basis.

Harold Harrison Associates will provide program services for numerical control of tooling to manufacturers in the United States.

Modern Data Inc. will specialize in database management systems using Clipper, serving small manufacturers throughout the state of Ohio.

Modern Data Inc. will provide clients in Ohio with staff training in database management systems using Clipper, offering seminars or other classes.

Modern Data Inc. will publish a monthly newsletter offering the latest information on Clipper and database management systems using it.

Start-Up Planning

Making a good start is essential. False starts cost time and money and are likely to cost you good clients. Take the time now, in advance, to anticipate the future and decide on your initial steps.

THE IMPORTANCE OF A GOOD BEGINNING

It was Aristotle who is reported to have said, "Well begun is half done," and he is reported by *Bartlett's* as having been quoting an older proverb. Thus it is evident that the wisdom of making a proper beginning is not a new revelation but quite an ancient one. Success in any new enterprise is difficult enough, of course, even with a faultless initiation, so it is well worth taking the time to plan carefully. We can find more than enough examples of ventures that were doomed to failure from the beginning because of bad planning. Some entrepreneurs manage to surmount a bad start and recover or start again, but it's a risky proposition. If bad planning results in a disastrous or abortive start-up, it may spell final and complete doom for the enterprise, whereas getting off on the right foot adds to your prospects for a successful venture. Planning should therefore begin with planning the start-up itself. In this chapter, we consider the items to think about and plan for before you hang out your shingle as a consultant

---

Things to Consider When Planning a Start-Up

- Services to offer
- Business location
- Business organization
- Choosing a business name
- Needed furniture fixtures, equipment
- Office supplies
- Basic marketing materials
- Administrative facilities and needs
- Short-term goals and objectives
- Special needs, if any
- Estimate of start-up costs

(see the box above). You made a start on planning some of these items when you worked on your mission statement, deciding what you will do as a consultant and how you will implement your ideas. Writing that statement required you to think about some of these items, services you will offer clients, for example. Let's consider that first.

SERVICES TO OFFER

You must start with a rather precise idea of the services you will offer. Granted that these services are defined as premises at this early time, and that you are likely to change them, perhaps even on a revolutionary scale, as your accumulating experience dictates. You need to be prepared to respond flexibly to the real market demands and market opportunities of the future, but in the meantime you must make some decisions, however tentative.

You decided in general terms when you wrote your mission statement(s) what services you will offer. There is the hazard of making your definition of services too narrow—overspecialized—and, so, constricting your market to a point where you will not have a broad enough range of business opportunities. Bear in mind that on the one hand you want a broad enough range of services to serve as a test program, enabling you to determine which services are well received and benefit you, as well as your clients, and which should be dropped. There is also the alternate hazard of offering too broad a range of services so that you are not focused. You must find a proper midpoint in which to position yourself. (Later, in discussing marketing, we will talk about the special meaning of "positioning" as something you work to create.) You can do so by first listing all the possible major functions of the field in which you will specialize, selecting those you think to be most salable, identifying those you most enjoy performing and those in which you believe yourself to be most expert. To illustrate this approach, let us suppose that you plan to open shop as a marketing consultant and offer appropriate services. But as is the case in most career fields and professions today, the range of functions and services is too broad to offer all. The functions of a marketing expert might include any or all the following:

Copywriting
Presentation design
Media selection
Promotional package design
Public relations/publicity
Speech writing
Campaign planning
Exhibit/trade show planning
List strategies and selection
Contest promotion and management
Convention management
Database management
Statistical analysis
Government contracting
Proposal writing
Market research

It isn't likely that you would want to do all of these, even if you felt capable of doing so. Certainly, it would be difficult to make a credible case of yourself as an expert in all these functions. Most prospective clients would be reluctant to accept you as someone equally expert in all these functions. They would be likely to see you as a jack-of-all trades in marketing or as an "I can do anything" kind of consultant. It is not an image that makes for success.

In fact, there are probably some of these many marketing functions with which you would feel less than completely comfortable because you don't enjoy the work or don't think yourself well enough experienced. That makes it easy to screen out those immediately.

What is left ought to be a few major functions so that you have the opportunity to compare results later to determine which are the best ones for you to choose as your focus. (I would make it a premise that where you start is not where you will finish.) However, the services ought to be related to each other. It would not make a lot of sense to present yourself as a specialist in convention management, copywriting, statistical analysis, and list strategies. Remember that this is not an irrevocable commitment. You will be reviewing results as you conduct your practice, and one day you will be making changes in your business plan and in your actual practice. It is likely that you will find conditions somewhat different than you expected, and you will have to be able to adjust to these.

I started consulting, for example, committed to proposal writing, and I expected to write proposals for clients, with their staffs providing the raw information input. I soon found out that if I wished to persuade prospects to agree to the daily fee I asked for my services, I would have to do more than write and, even more to the point, I would have to develop an *image* much broader and more sophisticated than that of "mere" writer. I would have to persuade my prospective clients to perceive me as a marketing expert (with special emphasis on government markets and contracts) who has the ability to implement those marketing skills in the written medium of formal proposals.

In the practical terms of the work itself and the specific services I provided, I would have to help clients analyze the requestor's needs, as expressed in their requests for proposals (RFP); develop strategies and solve problems; and even design their proposed programs, in many cases; lead and manage their proposal teams; and actually write and edit, too. I could never be stumped; I had to have an answer always, and I had to be creative. For example, the client's RFP might include a requirement for the successful contractor to train the customer's staff in use of the product the contractor was to manufacture. If the contractor did not have any capability for designing a training program, I had to design one to include in the proposal. In those and other such circumstances, I often designed, described, and wrote training presentations, personnel manuals, purchasing policies and procedures, report formats, presentation charts, fiscal policies, quality control plans, and numerous other items that originally I might have expected my client to supply. The true consultant manages to accomplish whatever needs to be accomplished to get his or her main job completed, and it is that ability that justifies a true consulting fee. Nominally, a consultant is a specialist, but you will, in fact, often find yourself a generalist, and that on the broadest scale imaginable.

Think, then, in planning the services you wish to offer how you wish to position yourself vis-à-vis client needs and what image you wish to project. Will you be narrowly or broadly focused? Just how broad a responsibility are you prepared to assume as a definition of the services you offer? How much will you gamble on your confidence that you can handle any and all of the relevant problems? At what point will some need become "not my job"?

Perhaps you can't answer these questions now, except to make certain assumptions, which you will later be reviewing as experience accumulates. Bear in mind, however, that what is true for others, even as "typical" or "average" truths, may not be true for you. Be prepared to be an individual, perhaps even an exception to the rule. Always bear in mind that consulting means dealing with unique problems, problems for which you must often invent new solutions spontaneously. Remember, too, that if clients and prospective clients do not have this image and this expectation of consultants' competence and capability generally, you will have to somehow help foster the development of this perception, if you want to be able to charge and get suitable fees.

BUSINESS LOCATION

You probably won't spend much time on deciding about your business location. The vast majority of independent consultants start their enterprises from an office in their homes, and most remain there, unless they begin to grow into a company with a number of employees.

You must consider the tax advantages of working at home, but remember that it must be dedicated space—used for business *only*—to be a legitimate business deduction. It's best to use an entire room or build an office in your garage or basement. If you cannot do this and must use some part of a room, put up a divider of some sort to separate it as an office, storage space, or whatever business facility it serves and use it for that business purpose only.

If you must take outside space for your office or for other business purposes, you will be well advised to start with something simple and inexpensive. You can generally lease or sublease a single office near home to keep travel time to a minimum, unless there is some business reason that compels you to locate at some other area. Many consultants spend most of their time on their clients' premises, and an office is primarily a place to keep files and a telephone answering machine, while others may spend a great deal of time in their own offices. Consider which is more likely to be the case when you are deciding where your office is to be.

BUSINESS ORGANIZATION

Beginning consultants tend to believe that there is some great advantage in being incorporated. That's not always true. In some cases it is advisable, in others anything but. The corporate shield protecting personal from business assets does offer some protection, and is worth considering if the consulting work you plan to do is such that clients are likely to hold you liable for anything that goes wrong and may sue you when things do not work out well for them. Remember that this has become a litigious society, and anyone can sue anyone else, even when the suit is unjustified. But incorporation is not a foolproof safeguard. It may (and may not) shield your personal possessions, but lawsuits will cost you money, even when you are incorporated and the lawsuit is without merit.

Liability insurance may be preferable to incorporation, if shielding yourself legally is your prime consideration with regard to the question of incorporating. However, it may be too expensive for you or may even be difficult to get. But consider it as an alternative and ask your insurance broker to advise you.

Incorporation adds paperwork and additional taxes, and under today's tax codes, it is doubtful if incorporation will save you much there. It is probably wise to consult a lawyer to discuss the pros and cons of incorporation per se and of the various types of corporations available to you.

If you operate as a sole proprietor, you need to do nothing much legally except check to see if there are any licenses the local government demands you buy. Some local governments have relevant licensing laws, but many do not. You will have to check at your city hall and county seat.

If you trade under an assumed or false name—ABC Services, for example—you will probably have to register as a "dba"—doing business as—entity, so that anyone wishing to find the proprietor of ABC Services can do so. The requirements for filing a dba vary somewhat from one jurisdiction to another, and you will have to find out what they are in your state, county, and/or city (see Chapter 4 for additional details). If you incorporate, you can use any name you wish, as long as no one else is already incorporated under that name.

CHOOSING A BUSINESS NAME

Another problem over which many consultants spend sleepless hours is that of choosing a business name. Many find the tendency to choose something imposing irresistible, and they wind up calling themselves something such as Data Systems Corporation of America or, if they are enamored of pronounceable acronyms, they will labor at producing something along the lines of Great American Data Systems (GADS). Again, that approach can have a reverse effect. One government executive I knew was fond of murmuring, "The bigger the name, the smaller the company," when some brochure or card crossed his desk bearing an impressively long name. There is nothing demeaning about trading under your own name, and it does not prevent you from winning contracts with large and prestigious organizations, even the federal government.

FURNITURE, FIXTURES, EQUIPMENT, AND SUPPLIES

The same considerations apply in planning your needs for furniture and related items. Unless there are compelling reasons to do otherwise, the sensible thing is to make do as much as possible. It's always easier to spend money than to earn it, and a computer program or training manual written at a makeshift desk salvaged from the attic is as valuable and as profitable as one written at a $1,500 mahogany beauty of a desk. (Even today, years later, I am still using book shelves I assembled from knockdown kits I bought at a local hardware store when I was starting.) This opportunity to economize is especially the case if you work at home and will rarely have a client visit you. Who, then, do you need to impress?

Make the rank order (1) salvage, improvise; (2) buy used, wherever you can find the best bargains; and (3) buy new, if unavoidable, but serviceable and inexpensive models. Also, buy the minimum kind and number of items now. Later, when you have revised your plans several times, you will have a better idea of what you need, and you may discard some of that with which you started.

In equipment, a desktop computer is almost indispensable today. Prices have fallen sharply, so do some comparison shopping and, if possible, consult a friend who has some relevant experience.

A fax machine is also a necessary item today, and is, fortunately, relatively inexpensive, except for the plain paper models. Many people prefer a fax board, which permits you to use your computer as a fax machine. The board is less expensive than a standalone fax machine but sometimes is not completely compatible with others' fax machines and offers a few other limitations. I believe you are better off with a standalone fax.

Unfortunately, many consultants make the mistake of investing heavily in office supplies. They tend to buy a huge quantity of expensive stationery and business cards, and otherwise make what usually prove to be erroneous estimates of their needs in this department. Don't be misled by the greatly reduced unit prices offered if you buy in quantities that would last you for several lifetimes. It's a false economy. Buy small quantities at your local office supply store. It's easy enough to get more when you need more.

BASIC MARKETING MATERIALS

Many consultants regard stationery and business cards as marketing materials, and they do have some utility in marketing. You do want to make a good impression on clients and anyone else to whom you hand your business card or write. But what is a "good impression?" Is it cards, letterheads, and envelopes on the most expensive papers, printed in several colors and with your photo printed on them? Is it an expensive, custom-designed logo embossed on all documents? (Yes, some consultants go to these extremes.) How far you go in an effort to impress clients and prospective clients is up to you, but overdoing it may have a reverse effect, as driving up to the client's office in a Jaguar or Rolls Royce might: The client may infer from viewing such a spectacle that retaining you means paying for your extravagant tastes with extraordinarily high rates.

You will probably need a brochure of some sort, describing what you do. The philosophy is the same: The brochure in simple good taste is not only as effective as the costly, glossy, and ostentatious one, but may very well be more effective than that extravagant model for the same reason.

ADMINISTRATIVE CONSIDERATIONS

Purchasing stationery and office supplies are minor administrative considerations, although many beginning entrepreneurs spend far more time and money on these items than is necessary or justified.

The same is true for furniture, fixtures, and equipment for the typical consulting practice, which normally is not capital intensive at all. Many other items necessary to the administration of the business are quite important. Insurance is one such item.

You need certain kinds of *insurance,* no matter what your business or how you have organized it. You need medical insurance for yourself and family today, when medical and hospital costs have risen to a point where even the medical group plans and the health maintenance organizations are having trouble staying afloat. You need casualty insurance to cover any possible casualty losses—by fire, burglary, storm, or other natural disaster. You need disability insurance to protect you and your family should you become ill or otherwise incapacitated for a long time. There is a good chance that in today's litigious milieu you need liability insurance, even if you have incorporated yourself. If you have entered into a partnership, you may decide that you need "partner insurance." That's insurance covering your partner's interest in the business, so that in the event of either partner passing, the surviving partner gets enough money to buy out the deceased partner's interest, which presumably has become the property of his or her family survivors. In that manner, having provided in the partnership agreement that a surviving partner has the right to buy out the interest of a deceased partner, the surviving partner is enabled to do so, thus preserving the business and preventing it from passing into the hands of a stranger of unknown business capabilities and acumen.

Accounting is a routine function, and yet it is a most important one, especially for a small, new business struggling to become established. The most important function of the accounting system is to keep you posted continuously, almost on a daily basis, on how the business is doing. It is far too easy to lose money and be unaware of it for a long time. A proper accounting system should make it so easy for you to be aware at all times of how you are doing that it is difficult for you to be unaware of it. You would do well to consider at least posting your own ledger so that you are always directly in touch with the important matter of "the numbers" of your business.

Should you decide to use a public accountant to handle your books and taxes, you probably will assume that your accountant is a tax expert, especially if he or she is a CPA (certified public accountant). That assumption may be unwarranted, despite the fact that your accountant will be glad to make out your tax returns. Not every CPA is a tax expert, nor is every lawyer a tax expert, as I learned through costly experience. Tax expertise has become a highly specialized field today. If you feel the need for a true tax expert, you will have to seek one out, probably by inquiring among business friends and acquaintances, or asking your lawyer. (An experienced lawyer is likely to know of a tax expert.)

SHORT-TERM GOALS AND OBJECTIVES

Your immediate objectives—for the first 90 to 180 days, that is—should be articulated here as the overall goal of the start-up. How much progress should you expect to make in 90 or 180 days (probably the latter, 90 days being a bit too short a time)? How long should it take you to win your first paying client? How long to win a second one? What should be the state of your affairs at the end of 180 days?

You may have started with a single client. Many independent consultants do, and, in fact, the reality of a guaranteed first client often inspires the launching of an independent consultancy. A single client is not a viable consulting practice. One mistake far too many beginning consultants make is to start with an excellent client and assume that when and if there comes a lull in that client's need, there will be ample time to begin marketing to start building a client list.

That assumption is a mistake, of course. It is too late to start marketing then, for in consulting, it usually takes time to build a clientele. Marketing activity pays off in results only weeks and, usually, months later. Set yourself goals of the number of clients you should have by the end of 180 days, 360 days, and so on. Keep those goals firmly in mind and work at meeting them.

ESTIMATE OF START-UP COSTS

It may be a surprise to you that estimating the start-up costs is placed last here, instead of up front. In fact, why is it here at all, since we started with the premise that your primary motive in writing a business plan is not raising capital but planning soundly. It is here because even if no large outlays are necessary, you will have to make at least some small investment to get started, and you need to face that.

I have placed this activity last because you need to have a look at everything you are likely to need before you can make a reasonable estimate of start-up costs. In fact, if you thought that you needed nothing more than business cards to get started, it may come now as a revelation to discover that launching a relatively simple venture such as independent consulting does involve some expense. You may already own an abundance of furniture and equipment suitable for your business start, but perhaps you have not considered all the costs—insurance, for example. Medical insurance alone is a major concern for the individual launching an independent enterprise, and liability insurance may be both difficult and expensive to get. You need to estimate the various start-up expenses and then sort and classify them according to priority, so that you do not sacrifice necessary and important items, such as insurance, in favor of items that would be nice to have but are not truly essential, such as a new desk.

NOW, THE NITTY-GRITTY

We have been looking at what is needed in a philosophical sense, taking a preliminary look at start-up planning. Now we are going to get down to cases. In the chapters to follow you will be asked to do some real planning, in specific detail, with worksheets offered to help you think things through.

4

Initial Commitments

There are pros and cons in every set of alternatives. The purpose of planning is to make the road ahead a bit easier by making the right initial choices and committing yourself to them by putting them in writing.

THE FORM OF ORGANIZATION: CHOICES AND CONSIDERATIONS

The basic premise of this book is that you, a typical reader, are an independent consultant, operating alone, or planning to operate in that manner. Still, you may be one of those who is planning to enter into a partnership with one or more other independent consultants. Such arrangements do exist. Worksheet 4.1 will help you think through the choices and reach some decisions. Study the alternatives, consider the possible cross-effects of each approach, and make your formal commitments, getting things down on paper. We start by considering the type of organization. There are, of course, the three basic approaches to business organization for permanent arrangements: sole proprietorship, partnership, incorporation; and joint venture for temporary arrangements.

Worksheet 4.1. Organizational planning.

1. The form of my business organization will be the following:

   ☐ Sole proprietorship   ☐ Incorporation
   ☐ Partnership   ☐ Joint venture

   My reasons for choosing this form: _____

   _____

   _____

2. If a sole proprietorship, I will trade under the following name:

   _____

   If using a name other than my own, as a sole proprietor, I will register the name properly with the local government authorities, as required by law.

3. If a partnership, the partnership will be between/among the following individuals:

   _____

   _____

   _____

   The lawyer I will engage to represent my interests in drawing up a partnership agreement will be:

   _____

   Listed are reasons for preferring partnership:

   - _____
   - _____
   - _____
   - _____

   My main strength(s) in the business will be:

   ☐ Technical knowledge and skills
   ☐ Marketing and sales:
        ☐ Experience   ☐ Contacts   ☐ Selling skills
   ☐ Related business experience
   ☐ _____
   ☐ _____

Worksheet 4.1.   Continued.

My partner will add the following strengths:

- ☐ Technical knowledge and skills
- ☐ Marketing and sales:
  - ☐ Experience   ☐ Contacts   ☐ Selling skills
- ☐ Related business experience
- ☐ _____
- ☐ _____

My partner and I have written a partnership agreement and have agreed to the following points:

- Percentages of capital and ownership
- Buy or sell agreement if one wants to get out of the partnership
- Ownership of partnership if one dies
- Assigned duties and responsibilities
- The name of the company will be: _____
  _____

4.   If incorporating, the type of corporation will be as follows:

- ☐ Close or family corporation
- ☐ Subchapter S corporation
- ☐ Nonprofit corporation

The name of the corporation will be:

_____

The attorney who will incorporate and advise me will be:

_____

There will be a limited number of shareholders and they are:

1. _____

2. _____

3. _____

4. _____

Worksheet 4.1.   Continued.

The following will serve as officers of the corporation:

President: _____

Vice President: _____

Secretary: _____

Treasurer: _____

The following will serve as directors of the corporation:

1. _____

2. _____

3. _____

4. _____

5.   If a joint venture, the name of the joint venture will be:

_____

The other party to the joint venture will be:

_____

_____

Sole Proprietorship

Studying Worksheet 4.1 may suggest to you not only that several options are available, but also what is involved in each option.

The sole proprietorship is the least complicated and least expensive form of business organization. There are no special taxes, fees, licenses, or agreements required, other than any licensing your local government might impose on you (which you would encounter, anyway, in any other form of organization). And there are no legal expenses in drawing up forms or other documents. As a sole proprietor, the company is you, and you are the company. You can and do make all decisions. You bear sole responsibility and sole control. If you choose to trade under your own name, you need not even register your business, except if there are local licensing rules you must follow or a local sales tax that applies to what you propose to do.

Doing business as.   If you choose to use a name other than your own in doing business, you probably must register that name under whatever "fictitious names" or similar statute exists in your state, county, and/or local government. In a few cases, no such statute exists, but those are exceptions. Moreover, in some cases, you must register your business name ("dba") with both your local and state government.

The purpose of that kind of statute is simple enough: It is to protect the public. That is, it enables others to discover who is the owner of "XYZ Consultants," should it be necessary to do so.

The procedure is usually simple enough: It involves registering your dba and your own name with the local or state government and may require advertising the fact for three days in the classified pages of a newspaper, announcing that you (your name) is doing business as (your business name). Figure 4.1 is an example of an affidavit that may be used to register a fictitious or dba name. It is based on a premise that the statutes of that jurisdiction require publication of a notice to do business under other than the owner's name, which is not the case in all jurisdictions. In fact, in some cases you may be furnished an official form to fill out, and not require making up a separate affidavit or having a notary seal.

Affidavit for Filing a Fictitious Business Name (DBA)

State of _____

County of _____

1. It is hereby stated, under oath, that the undersigned intends to engage in business under the following fictitious name and at the following address:

Name: _____

Address: _____

2. The full and true name of each person with an interest in the business and the ownership interest of each person is set forth below:

Name	Interest (Percentage)
_____	_____
_____	_____

3. Proof of publication of a notice of intention to do business under a fictitious name is filed herewith.

Dated: _____

/s/ _____ , owner /s/ _____ , owner

By: _____   By: _____
       (name of owner)   (name of owner)

On _____, 19____, the above parties appeared before me and, being duly sworn, did state that he/she/they is/are the owners of the business described in the above document and he/she/they signed the above document in my presence.

/s/ _____

Notary Public, for the County of _____   (seal)

State of _____

My commission expires _____

Figure 4.1.   Sample affidavit for filing a
fictitious business name (dba).

Partnership

Partnership is a possible choice if you are entering into a consulting practice with one or more other individuals. A simple partnership, with equal shares of duties and benefits, is the least complicated way of organizing a venture with one or more others, although that is a benefit of perhaps questionable merit, given the common difficulties of partnerships.

The advantages of partnerships include a broadening of technical knowledge and skills available to the practice and your clients—two heads instead of one to solve problems—an ability to handle larger projects than you might be willing to undertake alone, a greater ability to market—more contacts, perhaps—and a resource that enables each of you take time off when necessary without closing down the shop. These are not inconsiderable blessings.

Of course, there is a down side to this arrangement. Let us assume that you are equal partners with equal shares in everything, a common arrangement. It is easy enough to decide what are equal benefits, but it is often a problem to agree on what is an equal division of duties and responsibilities. Partnerships are often difficult because one partner is not satisfied that the other is carrying his or her share of the workload. Often enough, each partner thinks that he or she is doing most of the work and making most of the contribution to the business.

Thus it is especially important that these details of what each partner is to do are spelled out quite carefully in a formal agreement and that the agreement be signed quite willingly and not grudgingly by each partner. (No agreement is worth much if either of the parties enters into it reluctantly.) Without this condition, the future does not bode well for the partnership. Even when the partners have been firm friends previously or are closely related, this hazard exists. More than one firm friendship has been destroyed by entering into a business partnership. At the least, draw up a contract that provides for dissolution of the partnership by mutual consent or a buyout of one partner by the other. By all means, consult a lawyer about drawing up a partnership agreement to be sure that you have all the bases covered. One alternative is to engage a lawyer who is a stranger to both of you and is chosen by your mutual consent. However, if your partner-to-be wishes to have his or her own lawyer draw up the agreement, you should have your own lawyer present to protect your interests. No matter what the personal relationships with your partner-to-be are or have been, this is a business relationship, and you will be wise to be entirely businesslike about entering into it.

Figure 4.2 is an example of a simple partnership agreement, drawn up for a partnership of two people but easily adaptable to partnerships of more than two. In this example, relatively little is pinned down in advance, except to make it clear that the partnership is one of equal shares, with most matters to be settled through mutual agreement, rather than through predetermination. That is, no salaries are specified, nor even capital accounts, but merely drawing accounts, to be decided on later. Neither partner is committed for any specific duties, on the assumption that all matters can be handled amicably by conferring formally or informally with each other. You can add as many clauses to it as you wish to cover such contingencies as procedures for withdrawing from or ending the partnership, what happens if one of the partners dies, and other matters not covered in the example, such as the assignment of major duties and responsibilities of the partnership. If you don't cover all the bases in the original agreement, you can amend it later with added clauses. On the other hand, you can write completely separate agreements covering these matters. Each method is valid, but it is undoubtedly best to think everything out and cover all contingencies in the original agreement.

Is that a good way to handle partnership? Or should designations be made of responsibility for various duties—marketing, management, administration, and others? How much should be left to mutual agreement? How should disputes be resolved? (Bear in mind that the partnership agreement is a contract between two individuals, with normal considerations such as those governing all contracts and contractual relationships.) The premise upon which this agreement is based is that the partners will always be able to resolve differences of opinion by discussion, and that all the necessary duties of managing and marketing the business will somehow get done. That can be a risky assumption, and some thought ought to be given to it up front.

Partnership Agreement

Agreement entered into this _____ day of _____, 19_____
between _____ of _____, _____,
_____, _____, and _____ of
_____, _____, _____, _____, Partners.

1. Business Name. The parties hereby agree to form and conduct a consulting practice under the trade name of _____ .

2. Business Domicile. The partnership shall conduct its consulting business at _____, _____, _____, _____, and at such other places as the parties shall select or business requirements dictate.

3. Term of Agreement. The partnership shall continue until dissolved by mutual agreement.

4. Capitalization. The capital of the partnership shall be contributed in equal cash contributions by the Partners.

5. Division of Profits and Losses. The net profits of the partnership shall be divided equally between the Partners, and the net losses shall be borne equally by them.

6. Salaries. Neither Partner shall receive any regular salary for services rendered to the partnership, except as agreed upon mutually by the Partners subsequent to this Agreement.

7. Drawing Accounts. Each Partner shall be permitted a drawing account as may be agreed upon by both Partners.

8. Dedication of Efforts. Both Partners agree to devote their full time and attention to the business. The Partners shall have an equal voice in the management of the partnership business.

9. Ledgers and Records. The partnership accounts and records shall be kept at the place of business and shall be at all times open to inspection by either Partner.

Figure 4.2. Simple partnership agreement.

10. Funds on Deposit. All funds of the partnership shall be deposited in its trade name at the _____ Bank of _____, and all withdrawals therefrom are to be made upon checks signed by either partner.

11a. Voluntary Termination. Either Partner may withdraw from the partnership at any time by giving the other Partner _____ days' notice of his intention to do so. The remaining Partner shall have the right to either purchase the retiring Partners' interest or to terminate the partnership by liquidating the business. If the remaining Partner elects to purchase the interest of the retiring partner, the purchase price shall be equal to the book value of the retiring Partner's interest in the partnership business as reflected in the partnership books. The purchase shall be financed by payment in full or by an initial payment of $ _____, and the balance paid in installments over a period of _____ years, bearing interest on the unpaid balance at the rate of _____ percent per year.

11b. Involuntary Termination. Upon the death of either Partner, the surviving Partner shall have the right either to purchase the interest of the decedent in the partnership or to terminate and liquidate the partnership. If the surviving Partner elects to purchase the decedent's interest, the terms and conditions shall be those set forth in the preceding clause. If the surviving Partner does not elect to purchase the interest of the decedent in the partnership, he shall proceed with reasonable promptness to liquidate the partnership.

In Witness Whereof, the parties have signed this Agreement.

(Witness)　　　　　　　　　　　　　/s/ _____

　　　　　　　　　　　　　　　　　　　　John Doe

/s/ _____　　/s/ _____

　　　　　　　　　　　　　　　　　　　　Rob Roe

Figure 4.2.　Continued.

Failing to establish rules in advance can become an even more serious consideration if it happens that you expect the partnership to require some financing. A partnership means that the partners are equally liable for any debts and other obligations of the partnership. Before you assume equal responsibility for debt acquired in partnership, write a good agreement. You need a lawyer who represents you and your interest, and you need to discuss seriously with the lawyer any concerns you have.

Still another concern is the consequence of a breakup of the partnership. Suppose you each decide to go your separate ways: What happens to the records of the clientele? These are an asset of the business. Who keeps possession, or how do you settle the matter of how to dispose of these equitably? Do you sign some kind of noncompete agreement, or find some formula for dividing the client list? The problem is best considered up front, before making the commitment.

That is why space is provided on Worksheet 4.1 for you to think out why you prefer a partnership, if you do. I have presented several good reasons for being cautious about a partnership. But there are also reasons for embracing the idea of partnership. In any case, you will want to think out all the pros and cons in some detail before committing yourself to this serious step. The box on the following page includes some reasons you might think of. Note here that these reasons ought to mesh with the information you provide in those spaces of the worksheet calling on you to estimate your own strengths and those of a prospective partner. Use that information to make your analyses.

Incorporation

If you are considering a partnership, you ought to give serious thought to incorporating, especially if you are going to seek debt financing (borrowing money, rather than seeking investors). However, there are other reasons to opt for incorporation; it can offer other safeguards—against unwise partnerships and joint ventures, against your own impulses and unwarranted generosity, and, fre-

---

Reasons to Choose Partnership

Broadened capabilities. Perhaps you think that your own technical skills are not broad enough or great enough to support a consultancy, and you have a prospective partner of impressive skills and experience.

Increased marketing effectiveness. It may be that you are bearish about your own ability to market well and your prospective partner is quite strong in marketing ability and perhaps rich in "connections" and "contacts" for consulting contracts.

Complementing skills and experience. Perhaps you are both strong enough in skills and experience but your respective skills and experience complement each other synergistically so that together you have a greatly increased capability to offer clients.

Other considerations. There may be other, special considerations. (That is why blank spaces are provided on the worksheet.) Perhaps you both have established moonlight practices that you believe make a perfect combination now for full-time operation. Or perhaps one or both of you have some very special skills or experience that should open up special markets to you if you can present a strong image.

---

quently, against unanticipated events. I speak from sad personal experience in this. The fact that I insisted on incorporation in a partnership venture some years ago proved to be a wise precaution: It enabled me to retain full ownership of the intellectual property I had created earlier as a private individual. That property, a book manuscript, was to have been the nucleus of the venture, and clear title to it would have been clouded had I contributed it to an ordinary partnership or even a joint venture, rather than setting up a corporation and granting the corporation a limited license to use the property. Thus, when the partnership I had agreed to proved unworkable, I was able to withdraw my property and buy out my partner at a figure I could accommodate.

In this mode of partnership or joint venturing—that is, a separate corporate entity—you can control your personal commitment. A mutual buyout agreement usually means that you and your partner, who would presumably be the only shareholders, would be required to give each other the right to buy the other's share before either of you could offer your stock to anyone else.

Of course, you don't have to have a partner to form a corporation. You can not only form a corporation yourself, but in many states you can hold all the offices yourself. There are, however, various forms of incorporation. The most common for small business is the close or family corporation, but some consultants have expressed a fondness for the S corporate form, which avoids corporate taxes, the income passing through directly to the individual, who bears the tax liability personally. And there are still other forms, including that of nonprofit corporation. You should consult an experienced lawyer to discuss the alternatives here. The problems and potential problems of partnership exist also here to at least some degree and must be considered.

Joint Ventures

Partnership agreement or partnership via incorporation is presumably intended to be a permanent arrangement. There may be occasions when you wish to consider joint venturing, a temporary arrangement. It may be because you wish to undertake a project too large for you to handle alone or because the project calls for skills and other resources you cannot supply without turning to others. Of course, you might consider other ways to solve the problem—for example, using vendor services or hiring people—but decide against undertaking the risk and the probable management burden alone.

Or you may wish to enter into a joint venture with a prospective partner but want to put a working partnership to the test without committing yourself to it fully. This is one way of making a temporary working partnership to see how well you work together.

You should, of course, have an agreement drawn up between you. Figure 4.3 offers a rough model that can be adapted to your needs. It is for a joint venture between two parties, although it can easily be adapted to use as a joint venture among more than two parties.

There are several ways to approach this arrangement. One is a simple joint venture, conducted at the business address of one or both parties, or at a separate address that will be maintained for and by the joint venture. It makes sense to capitalize the joint venture, if possible, by mutual contributions, set up in a special fund.

The alternatives and possibilities for organizing the joint venture are many, for the situation is a flexible one. Normally, you would identify the joint venture as a new entity, albeit not a permanent one, with a name of its own and other attributes of a separate business entity. You can set that up as a company and enter into the joint venture as individuals. If you are incorporated, you can still enter into the joint venture as individuals, leaving your corporations uninvolved, or you can enter into the joint venture as corporate entities. Further, you can set up the joint venture as an ordinary company—a joint proprietorship—or you can incorporate the joint venture as a separate corporate entity.

The agreement set forth as Figure 4.3 assumes equal contributions by each party, but that is not a necessity to make the joint venture work. However, if the venture is not equally funded by the parties, presumably you will want to make adjustments of compensation and equity prorated in the amount of contribution. The parties in a joint venture do not have to have equal interests.

Whatever has been said about partnership agreements applies equally here, although the term of the agreement is temporary, rather than permanent. The hazards are the same, but the total effect of Murphy's Law striking a joint venture will probably not have as serious an effect on you as it would had it struck you in a full-blown partnership.

Joint Venture Agreement

Joint Venture Agreement entered into the _____ day of _____, 19_____ by and between _____ and _____ .

The Joint Venture shall conduct business under the name

_____

for the purpose of _____ .

The term of the Joint Venture shall be from this date until _____, 19_____ unless extended or ended sooner by joint agreement of the parties. The parties to the Joint Venture shall execute the necessary documents to register the Joint Venture properly with the relevant offices of the County of _____, State of _____ .

The Joint Venture shall be capitalized by equal contributions of $ _____ from each party, the total sum to de deposited in an account in the name of the Joint Venture in_____ .
Disbursements from that account shall be in the form of bank drafts, to be signed jointly by the authorized representative of each party.

Profits and losses of the Joint Venture shall be determined in accordance with good accounting practice, as reported by a CPA to be chosen by mutual agreement between the parties as accountant for the Joint Venture, and shall be shared equally between the parties.

_____ is named General Manager of the Joint Venture and shall have sole control of the conduct of the business of the Joint Venture, subject to review and approval by the parties.

The General Manager shall be paid $ _____ per _____ for the duration of the Joint Venture and shall be reimbursed for all reasonable expenses incurred in the performance of his duties.

Each of the parties shall be bound by any action taken by the General Manager in good faith under this Agreement. In no event shall either party be liable for any amount beyond the liability arising against him as a result of his capital contribution.

Figure 4.3. Joint venture agreement.

The relationship between the parties shall be limited to the performance of the terms and conditions of this Agreement. Nothing herein shall be construed to create a general partnership between the parties or to authorize either party Venturer to act as a general agent for another, or to permit either party to bind another other than as set forth in this Agreement.

Neither this Agreement nor any interest in the Joint Venture may be assigned, pledged, transferred or hypothecated without the prior written consent of the parties hereto.

This Agreement shall be governed by and interpreted under the laws of the State of _____. Any controversy or claim arising out of or relating to this Agreement or the breach thereof, shall be settled by arbitration in accordance with the Commercial Arbitration Rules of the American Arbitration Association in the City of _____, State of _____ and judgment upon the award rendered by the arbitrator(s) may be entered in any court having jurisdiction thereof.

Any and all notices to be given pursuant to or under this Agreement shall be sent to the party to whom the notice is addressed at the address of the Joint Venture and shall be sent Certified Mail, Return Receipt Requested.

This Agreement constitutes the entire agreement between the parties to the Joint Venture and supersedes all prior and contemporaneous agreements, representations, warranties and understandings of the parties. No supplement, modification or amendment of this Agreement shall be binding unless executed in writing by all the parties hereto. No waiver of any of the provisions of this Agreement shall be deemed, or shall constitute, a waiver of any other provision, whether similar or not similar, nor shall any waiver constitute a continuing waiver. No waiver shall be binding unless in writing signed by the party making the waiver.

/s/ _____   Date: _____

_____

/s/ _____   Date: _____

_____

Figure 4.3. Continued.

SIDE EFFECTS OF DECISIONS

In making each decision, you must consider how it will affect other decisions. For example, if you planned to operate your consultancy from an office at home but you decide also to enter into a partnership, where will you then locate your office? Will it be practicable to have it in either your home or your partner's home? If the partnership is on the basis of equal shares, how will you share the tax benefits of dedicating part of your home or your partner's home for business? With what other complications will you have to deal?

If you incorporate, together with a partner, other possible problems may arise. When you incorporate alone, it is often useful to make your spouse a corporate officer, such as vice president, secretary, or treasurer. That is difficult to do when you have a partner, who may wish his or her spouse to be an officer of the corporation. The two of you may have some difficulties in agreeing on these appointments. Again, partnership, even when incorporated, can lead to many problems.

Taxes and Bookkeeping

Taxes are, of course, a harsh fact of life today, and the filing of tax returns is a burden to everyone, especially to the small business-person. The extent of this burden is linked directly to some of the items we have just discussed. If you are an uncomplicated sole proprietorship trading under your own name, your tax returns are not a great deal more complex than are those of the typical wage earner, and it is practicable to handle your own taxes, especially if you have a computer and a suitable program. (Such programs are amply available.) Even so, you may prefer to have an accountant handle it for you; many do. If you are incorporated, your tax returns are considerably more complex, and it is even more likely that you will want an accountant to handle them.

If you are a sole proprietor, and even if you do not have a computer or are reluctant to try to run an accounting system on your computer, there are simple paper-and-pencil systems you can use. Usually, for the small one-person enterprise, the "books" are all contained in a single volume. There is contained in that single volume the log or day journal (sometimes referred to as a "diary") and the general ledger, along with payroll, tax forms, and instructions for their use.

Keeping books may become rather complex for the large corporation, but in principle it is quite simple, at least for the small business. The day journal is a running listing of expenditures, entered as they occur or as the bills arrive. Periodically—perhaps once a week or perhaps once a month—you transfer the information from the day journal to the general ledger. If you had three invoices for printing expenses—that is, three entries for printing expenses in the day journal for that week or month—you total them and post them in the ledger in the column you have reserved for printing expenses. You do the same thing with all other expenses. You then add each column to last week's or last month's entry, and you have a total for the year to date for printing and for every other class of expenses. Thus you can tell at any time what you have been spending for various kinds of costs. You do the same with income, of course, so you can tell how much business you have done in any given period and how much you have done for the year to date. This makes it easy to keep track of how you are doing, and how well reality tracks with your original estimates, as well as providing a direction for making quarterly estimated tax payments.

Not only do you then know how well you are doing, but you know where and how you are doing well or not doing well. That's the whole point of keeping books, other than for the tax collector: It's the feedback you need to monitor your business and make corrections to the course you are following when it is necessary to do so (as well as determine what corrections are needed).

Insurance

Even if you chose to incorporate and especially if you did not, you may need some kind of liability coverage, depending on the nature of the services you propose to offer. There is also the necessary casualty coverage for your records and equipment—burglary and fire insurance—and the medical coverage we all need today. That latter is itself a major concern for the individual entering upon an independent venture alone. It is a good idea to consult an experienced insurance broker to discuss what you will need here.

Contracts and Other Legal Concerns

Legal problems arise in every business. For one, there is the matter of contracts you will sign with clients. That is itself not a simple matter today, with both consultants and clients concerned about safeguarding confidential and proprietary information and other risks, resulting in noncompete clauses and numerous other contractual safeguards. It can easily become a treacherous morass to the lay person. You will want some form of legal service here.

This is another case where advance planning is important. The last thing you need when you are starting your business are legal problems. Unfortunately, it is quite easy to find yourself so embroiled. Many consultants operate on verbal understandings with clients—"handshake agreements"—and manage to run their businesses without difficulties thereby. On the other hand, many consultants have found it absolutely necessary to execute written contracts, even if they are rather simple ones, with their clients. (Some clients will insist on written contracts.)

There are preprinted "standard" contract forms readily available in stationers and office supply emporiums. There are books offering suggested contracts that may be modified. And there are computer programs that will turn out a contract with blanks for you to fill. These are all a help, but you are still a lay person, and you may need a lawyer to help you at least review a contract you have drafted with one of the kinds of aids listed here.

You can run into other legal problems, such as disputes with clients, problems with competitors, run-ins with local zoning laws, problems with licensing, or other items. It is a good idea to plan to do two things in preparation for possible problems:

1. Get a copy of the Uniform Commercial Code for your state. It's a basic law that pertains in all states but varies a little from

one to another, so you need to have the copy your state has adopted. Read it, but whether you do or do not read it in advance, keep a copy at hand in your office so that you can refer to it when and if necessary.

2. Know what lawyer you will call on, if and when you need legal counsel. When the need arises, it is too late to start looking for an attorney. Ask friends and acquaintances now for their recommendations and choose one or two lawyers as a resource to call on, if and as necessary.

PLANNING THE NEXT PHASE

As an independent consultant, you will probably handle most of administrative chores—ordering supplies, paying the telephone bill, and otherwise clearing paperwork from your desk—in whatever shards of time you can manage. There will be many such minor chores. The major and most important overhead (nonincome-producing) labor required of most independent consultants is that for managing, administering, and doing the marketing. To do that well, especially marketing, calls for good planning, and that is the subject we are going to tackle next.

5

Market Analysis

*Many a successful business has been built on the basis of a
founder's instincts, intuition, lucky guesstimates, and even lucky
accidents. Success sometimes comes in spite of such risky and irrational beginnings, but the odds are heavily against it. More often,
and far more reliably, success comes about as the result of careful
and thorough planning.*

THE ULTIMATE NICHE MARKET:
TOO GOOD TO BE TRUE?

A large conglomerate that employed me as an executive a number of
years ago designed and built custom automation/mechanization systems for client companies. One of these clients was a huge Canadian
candy manufacturer, who paid us more than a half-million 1965 U.S.
dollars to design and build an automated candy-packing machine.
Before the job was completed, one of our salesmen sold the idea to
another large candy manufacturer, and brought in an order for another machine. And soon after, another of our salesmen landed a
third order.

The company thereupon decided to build not two but five more machines, on what appeared to be a reasonable assumption that they had discovered a market and so there was ample reason to standardize the item and build some inventory for future sales.

Unfortunately, there were no more orders. Conducting belated market research, those in charge of our automation division learned that there were only six candy manufacturers in the world who had justification—that is, were large enough—to buy and use such a costly machine. We had captured half of that market already, an exaggerated case of a large frog in a very small puddle. Now we were stuck with three $500,000 useless modules of a system for which there were obviously extremely thin market prospects.

That is a sad tale of the consequences of failing to do market research or planning ahead. Unfortunately, executives in even the biggest corporations sometimes tend to shoot from the hip. Big or not, corporations are run by humans who make human judgments and human errors. But there is another significant message in that anecdote: Ironically, the story has its counterpart in the experience of many independent consultants who meet with instant success in winning their first clients. Of course, they read those painless marketing victories as meaning that either winning success in independent consulting is a snap or they infer that their clients find them irresistibly attractive as contractors. In truth, such sales conquests are a blessing later, when you are a seasoned veteran and recognize these strokes of good luck for what they are. When they happen at the beginning of your venture, they are often a disaster because they mislead you into neglecting to market aggressively, much less planning your marketing.

Again and again, I have seen new independent consulting ventures launched, only to have vanished from the scene a year or even less later when those early contracts were concluded and there were no more easy victories on the horizon. The failure rate is most germane here because a marketing plan is an integral and critically important element of your business plan. It is not a plan for some prospective banker, venture capitalist, or other investor; it is a plan for you, a plan to ensure success for your consulting practice.

WHO WILL BE YOUR CLIENTS?

In Chapter 2 I covered at some length the matter of defining your business, exploring the notion that all businesses are service businesses. You can define your business in more than one way, but the most effective and most insightful way to define it is in terms of what it *does* for your clients—or what clients *perceive* it as doing for them. But it is now time to move from the philosophical to the practical and see how this idea can be applied in devising and developing your market plans.

Your Market Is People

Recall the definition—definitions, in fact—of your business as being dependent on who wants to know and what his or her own interests are, as they affect their perception of what you offer. People and their wants ultimately define your business for you. "Ultimately," however, is after you have begun to do business and have an opportunity to learn what your clients want and do not want. Here we are talking about estimating and analyzing market possibilities, hypotheses or best guesses, that will have to be tested and probably altered to suit reality. But you must start somewhere, and there are two bases from which to emerge with your early plans.

A market can be, and is defined or identified in many ways, but a market is also, of course, people. It is people who make the decision to buy and who do the buying. Thus a first question may be this: Who will be your clients? That is, who are the people who are the best prospects for your services? What will they buy from you? Why will they buy from you?

Two Ways to Choose Your Prospects

You undoubtedly started with some idea of the kinds of services you would offer, for that is fundamental in the very idea of consulting.

You can decide arbitrarily, when you are in the planning stage, what kinds of services you wish to offer or feel best qualified to provide. If you start from that premise, you must identify your prospective clients by determining who is going to have need for and want to use the services you have decided to offer. If you take the opposite tack of deciding who the prospects are that you can or want to reach and sell to, then you will have to determine what their needs and wants are likely to be, and tailor your services to match those needs and wants.

Note that the basic choices are yours. You can decide what services you are going to sell and then define and seek out those who are most likely to want those services, *or* you can decide who you want to pursue as clients and then define and offer the services those clients will want. At the same time, recognize that there are limitations in both cases: You may or may not be in a good position to supply what you think clients are likely to want—that is, you must be sure that you can deliver what specific clients want. On the other hand, don't make the mistake my former employer did in selling $500,000 candy packers: Don't get too specialized in what you want to offer or there won't be a large enough market—enough prospective clients—for what you want to offer. In either case, be sure your offer is compatible with the size of the market and what the clients want.

In practice, you are most likely to start with the services you know best, those with which you have experience. You are likely to reason that this is what you can sell most easily because you are familiar with the market for those services and you feel reasonably at home in it. The fact is that, after the first year, few of us wind up doing what we thought we were going to do when we set out on our course. That change is why we have to review and revise our plans periodically. However, a necessary first step in preparing to write a marketing plan—that is, a marketing element of your business plan—is to develop two profiles. One is a profile of the kinds of services you will offer in terms of what problems or needs those services respond to, and the other is a working definition of the prospects for those services. Identifying the service should come first, probably, for the reasons stated, and then an analysis of who can use and will want those services can be made.

IDENTIFY THE SERVICE

Worksheet 5.1 is offered as an aid to help you make the relevant analyses and gain a clear view of your market—of whom your market consists, in fact. But first things first: It is necessary to get a clear idea of what it is you are going to sell by describing your services specifically in the next worksheet in the most concrete terms.

You Must Be Specific

First, list your major service or services, but not in vague generalities, such as "technical writing" or "computer support." The idea is to describe your service with what it *does* for the client in mind so that the service tends to explain itself. Also, avoid using all hyperbole, adjectives, and adverbs. Choose action words, and make them words with deeper and more expansive meaning than the impotent generalizations. Instead of putting "technical writing" on the worksheet, for example, you might say "Develop how-to manuals for computer software." "Develop" is a far better word than "write," in this case, implying a far more creative and helpful service than writing. Think about what that word "develop" means. But don't stop there. Try getting into the client's head: *Why* should the client want a how-to manual? What does it do for the client? What is the benefit? You need to know the answer to that question if you are to devise an effective approach to marketing, especially if you are to win against competitors who also write how-to manuals for clients. Remember always that you are a consultant, providing a custom service that includes analysis, creative development, and advising your clients.

Space is provided on the worksheet for all categories of information and estimates so that you may write in items not anticipated in designing the worksheet form or items of rare and exceptionally specialized services. For example, if you are willing to work under emergency conditions—on weekends and holidays and in late hours—be sure to note this point as a service. Later, you will use this and other special items in identifying the best prospects for your services, rou-

Worksheet 5.1.   What to sell and to whom.

---

1. Major service:

_____

Important amplification, if any:

_____

2. What it does for client:

   ☐ Solves problems   ☐ Cuts costs
   ☐ Adds value   ☐ Speeds operations
   ☐ Improves product   ☐ Enhances image
   ☐ Promotes sales   ☐ Generates publicity
   ☐ _____   ☐ _____
   ☐ _____   ☐ _____
   ☐ _____   ☐ _____

2. Additional major service, if any:

_____

Important amplification, if any:

_____

3. What it does for client:

   ☐ Solves problems   ☐ Cuts costs
   ☐ Adds value   ☐ Speeds operations
   ☐ Improves product   ☐ Enhances image
   ☐ Promotes sales   ☐ Generates publicity
   ☐ _____   ☐ _____
   ☐ _____   ☐ _____
   ☐ _____   ☐ _____

Worksheet 5.1.   Continued.

4. Product(s), if any:

    ☐ Newsletters   ☐ Audiotape sets
    ☐ Manuals   ☐ Reports
    ☐ Books   ☐ Software
    ☐ _____   ☐ _____
    ☐ _____   ☐ _____
    ☐ _____   ☐ _____

5. What it does (they do) for client:

    ☐ Solves problems   ☐ Cuts costs
    ☐ Adds value   ☐ Speeds operations
    ☐ Improves product   ☐ Enhances image
    ☐ Promotes sales   ☐ Generates publicity
    ☐ _____   ☐ _____
    ☐ _____   ☐ _____
    ☐ _____   ☐ _____

6. Who the users of such services/products (organizations) are:

    ☐ Software producers   ☐ Hardware manufacturers
    ☐ Service firms   ☐ Retailers
    ☐ Wholesalers   ☐ VAR dealers
    ☐ _____   ☐ _____
    ☐ _____   ☐ _____
    ☐ _____   ☐ _____

7. Who the buyers (for the organizations) are:

    ☐ Owners   ☐ Chief executive officers
    ☐ Purchasing agents   ☐ Comptrollers
    ☐ Production managers   ☐ Publications managers
    ☐ Sales/marketing managers   ☐ Proposal managers
    ☐ _____   ☐ _____
    ☐ _____   ☐ _____
    ☐ _____   ☐ _____

tine and special. If you offer seminars or other training services to clients, list this as a special service. (Obviously, these items can vary quite widely, from one consulting specialty to another.) Put a lot of thought into this area, for these items can make a substantial difference in your appeal. They may, for example, provide a distinguishing feature that makes your service unique or at least distinctive, and that can confer upon you a decisive feature vis-à-vis your competitors. Even one unique or unusual service can make the difference.

The True Need or Benefit Is Not Always Obvious— Even to the Client

The answer to *What is the true benefit of a how-to manual?* is simple enough: The how-to manual is not only a necessity—the client must provide such information with the product—but the perceived quality of the product itself depends on the quality of the manual. The client's customers usually have no way of judging the quality of a product except by how easily they can use it and how well it works for them. They don't really measure quality at all, in fact; they measure their satisfaction, and that depends largely on the quality of the instructions supplied.

Does your client understand that simple truth? Perhaps. Perhaps not. What seems to you to be painfully obvious is not necessarily as obvious or as well understood by your prospect. It may not be obvious at all to the client. Your prospective client may be supplying a how-to manual as an obligatory item, something customers expect but rarely use. Ergo, why spend more on creating it than necessary?

Prospects May Need to Be Educated

Because prospective clients often have tunnel vision, one thing you must do in marketing is to educate them. Make them understand why what you do is so important to them. Use the argument that their product is only as good as the manual, as far as the customer is concerned. Treat that as important information, as a revelation. Successful advertising does this regularly, painstakingly pointing out what you and I may think is obvious but which may not be obvious at all to readers, viewers, and listeners who have never really considered or analyzed the matter.

Does explaining the importance of what you do mean to a prospect that you will write a better manual than any of your many competitors? Strangely enough, for there is no direct logic in it, yes, it does suggest exactly that to prospects. Here is why: The fact that you point it out, whereas no competitor does (because competitors think it is too obvious a fact to require mentioning), suggests that only you understand the client's needs and problems, that you truly are a consultant and not just a writer. Thus the importance of analyzing the client's needs and identifying the direct benefit of your service becomes obvious.

What a Client *Really* Buys

You can assure yourself that you sell a service, that you sell a better how-to manual, that you sell the benefit of a better how-to manual—greater customer (the client's customer) satisfaction—and that is all true, and yet it misses the point, too. Whatever it is that you sell or think you are selling—better manuals, better service, happier client's customers—what the client is really buying is your *promise* of a better manual, a happier customer, and so on. That is all he or she can buy and that is all you can sell. Probably no client ever thinks of what he or she is buying in those terms, but that does not make it less true. Think of that when you make a presentation. The success of your sales effort depends on how convincing you are that you can and will deliver what you promise.

Understand Your Own Role

Of course, you are more than a writer when you do customer development of written materials. Are you not generally charged with the design and format of the manuals? Do you not make an independent analysis of the software and the user's needs in designing the manual and deciding what must be covered and how it must be covered?

The fact is that writing consultants do more than simply find words for their clients. Writing itself is the least part of the task. You must *develop*, perhaps even *invent* the manual for your clients, in most cases. (That has been my experience. Clients often need far more than they think they do or than they originally specified to you.) And you may very well need to have extended discussions with your client to answer questions, explain what you propose to do, and advise your client.

Of course, you are not going to go into all of that now in identifying what you do for your clients, but just find the words that will suggest the full import of what you do. Later, in a brochure or other marketing literature you create, you can explain more fully what "develop" or other significant terms you use mean, but for now, find the words that lay the groundwork.

Choose action words and active voice. Never "responsible for" or "assists" or "supports," but always some kind of "does" term—a word or set of words that denote aggressive and positive action. Don't "design" a security system; *create* one. Don't "study," "survey," or "research" the client's needs vis-à-vis whatever you are normally hired to do, but *find* or *identify* the need. Don't "hold orientation sessions" or "conduct training seminars" for the client's staff, but *instruct* or *train* the staff. Make your active, take-charge attitude clear. List your major service in such a term as to identify the *result* you will bring about with your service.

Focus on Important Items

How long the description of your services will be is up to you, but don't muddy the waters with a burst of trivia. The way to distill your description is to write out on a scratch sheet what you do in all the detail it takes to please you. Then edit the draft ruthlessly. Slash all the hyperbole—the adjectives and adverbs, especially the superlatives. Keep the main nouns but drop the minor ones. Come up, at the end, with only one to three major services. Cover them and support those expressions with details only as absolutely necessary. For example, my main service as a proposal consultant was to create a proposal that would be a major contender for the contract.

Amplifying detail would include strategy development and strong salesmanship in the presentation, but also troubleshooting and solving any and all problems that arise. That is important. As a consultant, I must be able to handle any problem that arises, and I must be competent to do so effectively or my credibility as a consultant fades rapidly.

For the small organization, I would usually write the entire proposal or most of it myself. For the large organization, I would expect contributions from the staff in-house, but I would probably lead the proposal team and do all the proposal management and coordination.

Most of us have one major service we provide, although we perform a great many tasks, some of them relatively menial, in carrying out the major tasks. But do not confuse the subordinate chores with the major service or services. Be sure you understand the difference and reflect it in your worksheet.

On the other hand, your offering may include more than one major service. Perhaps you also offer your services to develop other writing functions for clients, such as newsletters, press releases, speeches, and other items useful to clients for their publicity and public relations functions. In such case, again do an analysis and work out a client-oriented definition of the principal benefit—for example, promoting the client's sales, building or enhancing the client's image, widening the client's market, or providing other rewards for the client.

IDENTIFY THE CLIENTS

The considerations of benefits were preliminary to identifying your prospective clients, as already stipulated, before you profiled your clients. To carry on with the hypothetical example that you are a writing consultant, let's look at the section of Worksheet 5.1 that asks: Who are the users of such services?

The Organizations

A large number of writing consultants who specialize in developing technical manuals for clients focus their efforts on software developers, itself a large market that seems to be sorely in need of the services: Both software and hardware producers have become notorious for poor instructions in their manuals. (Quite often, the menus in the software are superior to the written instructions, but help menus are necessarily limited in the scope of their coverage.) Despite their in-house capabilities, there is an abundant market represented by manufacturers of many other kinds of products. Once, the writing chores were turned over to the design engineers, and they were expected to produce the manuals, but more and more today clients see the need for professional specialists to write manuals and perform other writing functions for them.

The two chief differentiating factors between those who need and seek outside help in writing their user instructions and those who do it in-house are the complexity of the product and the size of the organization. The sale of a radar system or a complex medical instrument would require a substantial manual normally, whereas the instructions for use of a VCR or electric can opener generally justify only a small pamphlet. On the other hand, even for an item of major technical scope and complexity, the large corporation is likely to have frequent need for writing services and therefore have in-house technical writers, while the smaller organization is more likely to seek consultant specialists when the need arises. Of course, there are exceptions to this "rule," and independent consultants may very well find it possible to win contracts with the largest corporations. That may be so because they need a specialist and do not have a suitable one on staff or they are already overloaded with work and need additional help. The latter is a fairly common condition.

Thus try to list here, in this section of your worksheet, the kinds of organizations for whom your services are likely to be attractive as helpful to them in some way—solving problems, reducing costs, and/or delivering benefits of other kinds.

That analysis must be in accordance with your chosen service area. If you wish to confine your activity to the local area, there is no point in listing prospects who are halfway across the country. Survey what kinds of organizations are in your area who are likely to have use for your kinds of services.

See the box below for reference suggestions. With such sources as these, it won't take long to build a prospect list, and to identify the several classes of prospective clients for listing in the worksheet—client *organizations*, that is.

Locating Organizations as Potential Clients

Newspaper help-wanted advertising. I have found this to be a rich source of information in building prospect lists of companies, especially high-tech companies. *The Wall Street Journal,* the Sunday *New York Times,* the *Washington Post,* and other major city dailies are all excellent sources for this.

Weekly tabloids. The several special weekly tabloids offer collections of the week's help-wanted advertising, usually available at any well stocked newsstand or magazine rack.

The trade journals and directories. You can find many of these in a large public library. But also ask your librarian for help. She can guide you to the *Thomas Register,* the Dun & Bradstreet *Million Dollar Directory, The National Directory of Addresses and Telephone Numbers,* and other useful sources of information.

Your local business club. Lions, Rotary, and other—and chamber of commerce. These organizations can often supply lists. Also, many county and state governments publish entire books full of information about local industry. Check on the availability of such books when you consult any of these organizations.

The People

Perhaps the organization is the other party to whatever contract you sign, and certainly they are going to pay your invoices, but you don't deal with "organizations"; you deal with people. It is people who read what you have written, listen to what you say, and decide whether or not to do business with you. And so it is people who are truly your clients, even if they do business with you in the roles they play in their organization. The next step (item 7) in making out the worksheet for planning your marketing is, therefore, deciding who are the people, in their roles, with whom you will have to do business.

This category varies with organizations, as a result of size—for example, only the large organization has a separate purchasing agent, but even the large organization may not have a purchasing agent if purchasing is not a major function within the organization and thus does not justify a full-time position. Even when purchasing is a major function, it is not always centralized: Some organizations authorize each department head to do his or her own purchasing. That is essentially the case in federal government agencies, with only rare exceptions. In state and local governments, however, there is a strong tendency to centralize all purchasing in a purchasing and supply agency or department, but even here, some state and local governments delegate a few classes of purchasing, including consulting, to agency heads.

It is important to know these things about the *people* who are your prospective clients if you are to market effectively. There is no way you are going to know all this up front, now, when you are drafting your plans, but be aware that finding out whom your contact should be is a goal you ought to set yourself for the future, as you build your lists of clients and prospective clients. Gather such detailed information, bit by bit, and develop a profile of each client and prospective client, thus developing a marketing database. It is a truism that it is the individual person, not the organization, who is your client. You can fail to win contracts with an organization over many tries, due solely to the fact that you don't know who to approach, whereas the sale can be an easy one when you approach the right person. In "knocking on doors"—cold calling on government agencies—I found that hours invested in searching out the right party to approach often produced a contract in a few minutes. Today, with our many means for gathering data at our desks via computers and fax machines, we can do much of the legwork without racing about physically, as we once did.

A WORD ABOUT THE WORKSHEETS

The worksheets contained herein are important because they will help you become aware of the kinds of information that will help you to succeed. You may be able to check off many items immediately, but don't do so too hastily unless you are sure of your answers. The items are there to be checked off with reliable information, not guesses. Take the time and go to the trouble of searching out as many answers as you can immediately, but don't abandon the blanks. You can fill these out later, when you have gotten the right information.

The worksheets in this and subsequent chapters are also useful for guiding the design of your *marketing database*. They suggest the fields you need in your records, fields that will enable you to sort your records and retrieve them selectively or address them properly when you wish to send out a sales letter, brochure, or proposal.

6

Analyzing and Qualifying Markets and Segments

We have long embraced the qualifying of prospects as a necessity of marketing. Today we are becoming more and more selective in identifying markets and, especially, niches as a more intensive and more discriminating kind of qualification.

QUALIFYING YOUR PROSPECTS

The term *marketing database* was not used carelessly or by chance in concluding the previous chapter; it was a deliberate choice. Marketing has always been a major cost in business, and qualifying prospects has been especially important—a necessity—in those fields where marketing requires intensive effort to close each sale. Consulting is not a "one call business"; it generally takes intensive marketing, often multiple sales calls or sales efforts to win clients. That means it usually requires presentations of one sort or another, from informal sales calls on prospects to formal proposals and perhaps even a "dog and pony show"—formal presentations in clients' conference rooms.

The requirement for presentations means, in turn, that you must qualify your prospects to be sure that you are not wasting your time in making follow-up calls and other sales efforts by addressing them to the wrong prospects, to prospects who are exceedingly unlikely to become clients. The concept of marketing databases—detailed profiles of clients and prospective clients—is a giant step toward achieving this selectiveness, and with today's technology it has become a practical reality for even the independent consultant.

The detailed profiles of each individual client and prospective client in database files is used to implement what is known as *databased marketing.* This is highly focused marketing by selecting clients and prospects whose profiles make them especially well suited for whatever you wish to offer. If, for example, you are a security consultant specializing in physical plant security and you have some new security system you wish to offer clients, you might set up a search of your database to find those whose security systems are aging, those who have suffered break-ins and burglaries, those whose offices or plants are especially vulnerable or especially attractive to burglars.

That is targeting your marketing, but it is also a means of qualifying your prospects so that you do not waste your time and money appealing to those who are not likely to buy your system, perhaps because they have recently installed new security systems or because the danger of break-ins is slight in their cases.

The general idea behind qualifying each prospect is, of course, to avoid time- and money-wasting efforts selling to prospects who are not truly interested in what you offer or who lack the money or authority to buy, in any case. The wise marketer therefore takes whatever steps necessary to establish the relevant facts before investing more than minimal time and money in the sales effort.

Marketing has become increasingly expensive, and even mass marketers pursuing sales of lesser magnitude are turning to improved methods of qualifying not only prospects but markets. Thus "targeting" is both a more selective choice of markets and niches to be pursued and a modern, improved method for qualifying markets, as well as individual prospects.

QUALIFYING YOUR MARKETS AND NICHES

Marketing, for the beginning independent consultant, is not only a most important element for success, but is also often the most difficult problem. As a new entrant to the field, you have no track record as an independent consultant. You may be able to furnish references who will verify your technical abilities and related work experience, but you are totally lacking in past and current clients whom you can cite as credentials. At best, even when you have become established to some degree, you may very well find it necessary to devote from 25 percent to 33 percent of your time to marketing. (Many independent consultants base their rates on the expectation of being able to bill not more than twenty hours per week.) In such circumstances, you must find means for ensuring that you put that time to best possible use by investing it in marketing only to well-qualified prospects.

Worksheet 5.1 made a good beginning in pursuit of that goal by profiling your prospective clients in general terms—that is, in the abstract. But now it's time to go to the next step: Instead of qualifying prospects, in this chapter we pursue the means for qualifying markets and market niches, especially the latter, since they ought to be of especial importance to any independent practitioner. A niche market you discover may prove to be a major asset, good for many consulting contracts, but it also may be prove useful for only an occasional sale. In that case, you do not wish to invest a great deal of time and money in it. Thus, it is important to have some means for determining how much effort is justified to mine any given market or niche, for determining what the true market potential of that niche is for you and what you have to offer.

Take careful note of that latter qualification: The objective is to evaluate the size of the market you have perceived only in terms of your own interest. I recall my employer once urging me to pursue business with the then new U.S. Department of Transportation. His enthusiasm for this potential market was based on the huge budget announced for the agency. A study of the agency and its budget, however, revealed that the bulk of its budget was to be devoted to third-party services—to subsidizing state and local governments in improving their transportation systems and facilities. Relatively little was to be available to contract for the kinds of services our company provided. Despite much marketing effort stubbornly expended there, we won only a small amount of business, certainly not enough to justify the effort.

Targeting overall goals as a one-person venture, you can aim to capture a small share of a large market or a large share of a small or niche market. Practitioners have been successful with both approaches. You may even be fortunate enough to discover a niche market of which no one else has yet become aware and thus capture the lion's share of it—perhaps all of it. Some entrepreneurs discover profitable niches only after being in business for some time, while others launch their enterprises on the basis of specializing in one or more niche markets perceived in advance. My own primary market for my consulting services was constituted originally by those companies who wanted to market to the federal government such services that were usually contracted for with companies submitting the most persuasive proposals, rather than the lowest prices. The ability to write top-notch proposals was and is, thus, an absolute necessity to be successful in selling many kinds of goods and services to government agencies. My principal niche was therefore constituted by those organizations in need of support in proposal development. (In some cases the prospects were aware of that need for support; in others, it was necessary to educate them, to do whatever would make them aware that they needed expert help.)

After a time, having settled into the niche and having begun to develop some reputation and references, I expanded into another niche that could perhaps be considered a subset of my original niche: the presentation of training seminars in proposal writing.

Over the years, I also found other niche markets. Where originally my marketing premises led me to target those for-profit companies in high-tech industries, I soon learned that associations and colleges were also good prospects for proposal-writing seminars. They became good prospects for seminars, that is, after I failed to win contracts resulting from the first few invitations to quote to them and learned what it took to win the contracts from them. Again and again I found that the premises that appeared to be so reasonable were false and had to be adjusted drastically, in the face of experience. Do not allow yourself to become unduly fond of your early premises.

Eventually I developed ancillary products, as well as ancillary services, including a newsletter, several manuals, and a number of special reports, all related to this niche, and all mutually supporting elements of my practice.

All of this activity was spontaneous growth, unplanned and therefore carried out far less efficiently than it should have been, had I made the effort to think things through and plan all the potential niches in my chosen market, or at least actually drafted the premises and deliberately tested them. Discovering that your theories and premises are wrong should never be a surprise; they ought to be the objectively observed results of deliberate validation tests.

A niche is a small segment of a market that perhaps has been neglected by major firms as being too small a segment to justify their marketing to it, perhaps has been overlooked by your competitors, or perhaps is truly too small to merit diversion of the marketing resources of even a one-person venture.

A niche may or may not prove large enough to support a full-time practice and provide potential for growth. The company I referred to earlier in a story about their candy packing machine had found a niche, but the niche proved far too small to support the company's expansion into the specialized field the niche represented. Niche marketing can be worthwhile, but it is a double-edged proposition: Niches can prove to be dead-end streets, as far as growth and expansion are concerned, and so should be approached with caution. Thus you may discover a niche, and you may do some business with even a shallow or narrow niche, but be careful about committing resources to it without some assurance that it is a market with enough potential to merit such a commitment.

REFINING YOUR ANALYSIS

In the previous chapter, you were asked to use a worksheet that called for making some rough estimates of potential markets, primarily identifying types of industries or organizations and individuals within the organizations to whom you would address appeals for business. These were, of course, your own estimates, based on whatever you know about the kind of service you offer and the organizations you believe to be your best prospects. You were not asked to do more, at that point, than make these estimates based on whatever thoughts you may have.

Now, with Worksheet 6.1, you are going to take a look at these estimates and start doing some logical analysis, to see how your original estimates stand up to such critical review. This activity should help you refine and detail these early estimates to begin qualifying your market prospects or, at least, to make preparations to qualify them.

The idea is to begin at least a preliminary qualification of each market and each market segment or niche you expect to address with your offers. You must qualify them along two parameters: Their suitability in terms of their needs, problems, and interests as matching or complementing the specialties you offer; and their size, as meriting the commitment of your marketing resources.

For each market or niche, make the best estimate you can of the match of the market to what you offer by describing, as best you can, the functions, needs, or problems typical of the companies referred to as those items relate to what you offer. If, for example, you are a computer consultant, what are the probable computer needs, uses, and problems of typical companies in that market: Database needs? Networks? Inventory management? Other? Estimate the size of the market in the only terms meaningful for your marketing needs: the number of potential clients.

Depending on what kind of consulting work you do, you may be looking at horizontal or vertical markets. That is, the markets may have nothing in common but the kind of needs that are relevant to your work—that is, each market may span various industries. (All kinds of companies may need to network their desktop computers, regardless of their industry.) Then there are vertical markets. It may be that you specialize in a service where most of your potential clients are in a single industry, such as banking or accounting. That doesn't matter. The only thing that matters is the commonality of their needs that require your services and your identification of that common factor.

Worksheet 6.1.   Analyzing and qualifying your market(s).

1. General description of main market(s):
   a.
   b.
   c.
   d.
   e.

2. Estimated size of each main market:

   Relevant Needs/Problems   Potential Number of Clients
   a. _____   _____
   b. _____   _____
   c. _____   _____
   d. _____   _____
   e. _____   _____

3. General description of niche market(s):
   a.
   b.
   c.
   d.
   e.

4. List/describe factors that distinguish each market segment or niche:
   a.
   b.
   c.
   d.
   e.

5. Estimated size/potential of each niche market:

   Relevant Needs/Problems   Potential Number of Clients
   a. _____   _____
   b. _____   _____
   c. _____   _____
   d. _____   _____
   e. _____   _____

For Example

The first item on Worksheet 6.1 calls for a general description of your main market or markets, as your market prospects appear to you now. There is no single best or correct way to do this. Depending on the kind of service you offer and other variables, a general description may call for identifying an industry, a type of company or other organization, or a function within an organization. Let us suppose, for example, that you are a copywriter and your specialty is direct mail. Almost any industry and company might logically be a prospect, but that is far too large a universe to address. If you used such a broad brush to make your original estimate in working out the previous worksheet, here is an opportunity to have another look at those entrants and narrow them down a bit. To illustrate the rationale, let's consider first just a few types of organizations who might be prospects for you:

Small appliance manufacturers
Food processors
Associations
Political parties
Banks
Oil companies
Distillers
Book clubs
Periodical publishers
Book publishers
Government agencies

Each of these represents a rather large universe in itself, but presumably you have been working in the industry and have a fair idea of where—in what industries, companies, and departments—you stand a fair chance of winning clients, and can so do some initial screening based on that knowledge and experience. Aside from that, it is possible to begin screening candidates immediately, based on what each is most likely to do in direct mail, if they get into it at all, and what you feel comfortable in writing. Here, for example, are some preliminary appraisals:

Unless you are experienced in fund-raising, recruitment, or vote-getting programs, you can probably eliminate political parties immediately. Political parties usually turn to direct mail only to solicit funds, voluntary workers, and votes.

Manufacturers of most hard goods do not often get into direct mail themselves, unless they are quite large, but even then they are most likely to rely on their advertising agencies for help, and are probably not good candidates for you. Manufacturers of soft goods and other items sold commonly in supermarkets often do get into direct mail promotions, however, and may be worth considering.

Banks get into direct mail, soliciting subscribers and credit card accounts. Banks tend to rely on vendors to create and run their direct mail campaigns.

Oil companies' direct mail solicitations are most likely to be similar to that of the banks, seeking applicants for their credit cards. As banks do, they are likely to rely on advertising agencies and other outside services to design and run their campaigns.

There is also the possibility that you can interest some organizations in starting in direct mail. You may wish to consider as prospective market niches organizations that ought to be in direct mail but are not, probably because it has not occurred to them or they don't know how to make a beginning in direct mail. (Something very much like this was the case in my own practice, in which I often helped firms, even quite large ones, launch themselves into marketing to government agencies for the first time.)

In my own case, I had gained most of my relevant experience in writing proposals and winning government contracts while I worked in electronics companies doing defense work. These were the kinds of companies I knew best. I thus started, almost unavoidably, with the premise that this was the industry and these were the kinds of companies I should address as my main market. I did, indeed, eventually win substantial contracts with such companies, but I found software developers much more receptive to what I offered. I found also, to my surprise, that some government agencies were eager to hire me to lecture to government employees on the subject of procurement and government contracts. In time, I learned that it was not only in my field of consulting activities that federal agencies hire contractors to train government employees in the business of government. Federal, state, and local governments depend far more on private-sector contractors than most people realize. Regardless of your field, keep the government markets in mind when evaluating your prospects. (Yes, government agencies have used direct mail to help carry out some of their programs.) But that is not the only surprise I received in the form of clients I would never have expected to have call on me. For one assignment, I journeyed to Jacksonville, Florida, to deliver a proposal-writing seminar to a large roomful of Salvation Army executives who wished to pursue and win halfway-house contracts from government agencies. In another case, a large hospital called on me to help them prepare a grant proposal to train doctors in what is now called "family medicine."

Targeting by Function

In some cases, identifying a general type of organization is sufficient to indicate a target market. In other cases, that is far too broad, and you must identify markets by function or by something that distinguishes the company. Most organizations, other than very small ones, are subdivided functionally, and your service might be welcomed and result in a contract only if your appeal reaches the right department or functionary in the organization. For that reason, markets are best identified in terms of users, those who would benefit from your services.

If you are a training specialist, you would identify those companies and other organizations who conduct training, regardless of their industries, but you should define the market as training departments. Be aware, however, that there is no single term that would identify the center of the function universally. It might be called training department in one organization, but the responsibility might fall on the personnel department in another, or be an ad hoc function of a production supervisor in still another. Then again, you may have organizations who develop training programs for client companies, and they might be potential clients for you also.

It is thus often a difficult matter to identify or define markets, and the full lists can only be built rather laboriously through a great deal of digging for information (via joining associations, studying advertising, networking, and doing other activities, for example) and growing experience.

Eventually, you will find it wise to establish a special database file with this information. You may then keep building and refining that file as you become aware of more and more markets and market niches. You add these to your lists—to your database files—and re-fine these early estimates continually with the new information and the resulting more accurate estimates. This information will ulti-mately prove to be an exceptionally valuable marketing asset. It is thus a good idea to bear this probability in mind now, and even to start your database now.

DESIGNING THE DATABASE

There are many database management programs (dbm) available, of varying levels of sophistication, size, and capabilities. There are two basic types, although there are hybrids and variants of each, in the flat file dbm and the relational dbm. The flat file dbm is the simpler model. The relational database is much more sophisticated and of-fers advantages of use, such as the ability to combine data from sev-eral files, as well as flexibility.

The dbm is actually a kind of shell that you can shape and mold to your own needs and purposes. In fact, you must design your data-base to suit your own needs, and it would not be premature to start doing so now, or at least to have your database needs in mind as you make entries in the worksheets.

Files, Records, and Fields

A database file is made up of a number of *records*, and each record is made up of a number of *fields*. Figure 6.1A is a simplified example to illustrate this composition. Each of the nine items listed—name, address, city/st/zip—is a field, and the set of fields is a record, all about the Jones Tool & Die Co. This is a very much simplified example, having only nine fields. If this were a database file for a mail order campaign, there would be many more fields, along the lines of Figure 6.1B.

The fields are also the way you find individual entries. If you couldn't remember the name of the company, but you had its telephone number or fax number, you could search out the record rather quickly, as long as that number occupied its own field in the record.

You design each database file to contain the information you need, but you also design it to be able to retrieve that information easily. Files are sorted by fields and records are retrieved by fields. Files are also searched by fields. If you wanted a list of all records in the zip code area 55555, you couldn't get it from a database file designed as is the one in Figure 6.1 because in that file the zip code is not a separate field. Therefore, one thing you must bear in mind in designing a database file is how you will want to retrieve records. Once you have built a large database of thousands of records, it is difficult to go back and change the structure. It would mean reentering every record. So even if you do not now anticipate that you will ever want to retrieve records by cities, states, telephone exchanges, or other such single items, it is safer to enter each into its own field.

It is not strictly true that you will not be able to search out a record by a bit of data that does not have a field of its own. There are search programs that will search for a single telephone number or name. Such a program is convenient and has its uses, but it is a clumsy and less-than-satisfactory substitute for a well-designed database in which you can sort, retrieve, make up lists, do analyses, and write reports without resorting to other special programs.

The model of Figure 6.1B is along the right lines for retrieval facility, although it is a skeleton set of fields: You will probably want many more to furnish a maximum marketing asset. Far better to have too many than too few, and there is small probability that you will have too many. You can sort and retrieve by any parameter or set of parameters. Perhaps you will want to develop a list of all on your list who use spreadsheets, but only those within a given zip code. Prob-

Name: Jones Tool & Die Co.
Address: 311 Industrial Hwy N.
City/St/Zip: Steel City, OH 55555
Tel: 555-7789
Fax: 555-7790
CEO:
Purchasing agent:
Production manager:
Engineering manager:
Main Prod/Srvc: Welding positioners
Contact: James W. Gruner, purchasing agent
Relevant needs: Inventory management, purchasing
Notes:

Figure 6.1A.   Simple record in a database file.

Name:
Address:
City:
State:
Zip:
Tel:
Fax:
CEO:
Purchasing agent:
Production manager:
Main Prod/Srvc:
Contact:
Interests:
Relevant needs:
Notes:

Figure 6.1B.   Slightly more sophisticated record.

ably, for your purposes, the most important fields are those in which you identify the principal product or service and the needs of the prospect or client. If, for example, you want to offer clients a new service or product, you can use these two fields to select the best prospects. However, these are still rather general fields, and you would probably do well to have several fields of prospects' products, services, and needs in highly specific terms. In my own case, had such facilities been available to me when I was hungrily pursuing clients, my database files would have probably included fields for such items as these:

Electronics engineering
Weapons systems engineering
Communications systems
Computer systems
Defense contracting
Publications department
Internal proposal writing group
Nonprofit organization
Membership organization

Any given organization might have met most, few, or even none of these qualifications, and so a search might retrieve many hundreds or even thousands of names, or only a handful.

You could easily have several thousand names in your database files, but have only a few hundred that are true prospects for your new item. Even among that few hundred, you might want to prioritize them in some declining order of estimated probability as potential buyers of the new item.

The notes field is one for entering other related items, perhaps a record of past contracts with them or special notes for winning their business again. As in the case of the other fields, you can make these as many lines long as you wish to allow ample room for information to be entered.

You probably will not have a great deal of use for some of these fields, but just as you never have too much computer memory and storage, you never have too many fields. The more fields you have, the more sorting you can do—in fact, the more *sophisticated* your sorting and report-writing capabilities will be. No matter how many you provide initially, you are quite likely to wish later that you had provided a few more. It is probably a wise idea to create a couple of blank fields, no matter how many you start with, to facilitate later additions. Bear in mind that you will need these fields if you want to target your marketing properly, for to do that you must collect a great deal of data that identifies and describes the interests, problems, and needs of each client and prospective client. That data constitutes the basis for databased marketing. Eventually, that data will enable you to develop profiles of the best prospects for your services, thus vastly improving your prospecting programs.

7

The Marketing Plan

Marketing for the consultant is a process of discrete steps, quite amenable to advance planning and always most efficient and most successful when planned carefully.

THE MARKETING PROCESS

Marketing is many things, but in the end it is whatever it takes to find or create an acceptable product or service, bring it to market, make the buying public aware of it and of its availability, and persuade enough people to buy it so that the business succeeds. It involves a series of distinct steps—I see it as a five-step process—that are nominally serial or sequential in their logical order, but with some qualifications:

1. Identify a marketable service or item.
2. Identify the most likely buyers, those individuals for whom the items should have the greatest appeal.
3. Identify the basic means for reaching these buyers (that is, market access) with your sales presentation.
4. Design the offer and proposition.

5. Design the marketing campaign—every facet, medium, approach, and means for presenting the offer and proposition to that population of most likely buyers.

One caution: The five steps are stated as though they were absolutes, each susceptible to being carried out in its own way, on its own terms, and independently of each other. Even the graphic representation of Figure 7.1 suggests this independence of each step or phase. In fact, they are not independent: There is a great deal of interdependence among these steps because the steps must fit together and complement each other, resulting in a viable pattern overall. The marketing campaign must thus have coherence as a process. Ideally, that coherence produces a synergy, a result that is greater than the simple sum of the parts. That happens when the various elements not only are compatible with each other but when they reinforce and add strength to each other.

For example, can you carry out step 1 without regard to step 2? Or even to step 3? That is, how can you evaluate the marketability of an item without considering who are most likely to buy the item? But what good does it do to settle on steps 1 and 2 without considering step 3: Can you reach the people of step 2 with news of the item in step 1? Suppose, for example, that you are trying to sell a service useful only to rocket scientists. Can you somehow find a large

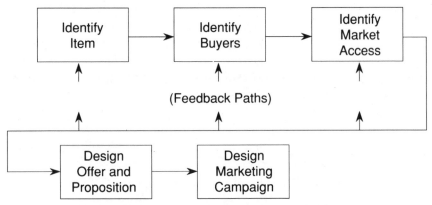

Figure 7.1.   Five major steps in marketing.

enough population of rocket scientists and reach them with your sales appeal? If you cannot do so—cannot gain access to your chosen market, that is—it doesn't matter how well you have identified the market or how ideal your service is, does it? (On the other hand, even if you can reach that potential and perhaps even merely hypothetical market of rocket scientists, are there enough rocket scientists to make a market of useful size?)

Thus the process is more cyclical than sequential. You go through the steps tentatively and go back to adjust your plans according to what you experience. This is illustrated in Figure 7.1 by the arrows that indicate feedback paths. Every step in the process produces new information, and that may cause you to turn back and modify some earlier parts of your plan. You may find, for example, that the buyers you selected as your best prospects are not your best prospects at all, but some other class of individuals is a better one for you. The idea is to do this analysis and planning up front, before you have committed major efforts and money to your marketing campaign. The failure to do so is not a disease peculiar to small business: Even the largest businesses have made major marketing blunders by failing to do adequate research and planning before committing their resources. The Ford Motor Company's Edsel is an outstanding example of such failure and, perhaps, of basing marketing decisions on wishful thinking, but there have been many others.

A MARKETABLE SERVICE

It is time to think seriously about the main service or services you will offer clients by referring to the notes you made on Worksheet 5.1. The general requirements your elected service will have to meet are these:

1. It must be a service you are well equipped to deliver.
2. It must be a service you are comfortable with.
3. It must be a service that is marketable.

Presumably, everything is marketable. In practice, some things are far more marketable than others. Following are a few examples, using familiar products to make the point, although the observation is no less true of services and their marketability.

Factors Affecting Marketability

Miniskirts were a great success, variations far less so, and maxicoats almost as lamentable a disaster in the "rag trade" (garment industry) as the Nehru jacket. Gary Dahl enjoyed great success with his Pet Rocks, hardly any with some other items he tried. Ken Hakuta, highly successful with his "wallwalker" toy, has so far been unable to achieve another success approaching this first one, despite many tries, many TV appearances, many rationalizations, and much preaching and writing (including a book) about how anyone can also become a great success in the toy and novelty business.

Be prepared in marketing to be wrong and to be surprised on occasion. Many things affect that quality of marketability, some of them entirely unpredictable. Timing may affect marketability, for one: There is often a right time for an item, a time when conditions are conducive to its success, just as there is a wrong time, a time when conditions conspire to prevent success. There was a great boom market for consultants in education and social sciences generally during the years of Lyndon Johnson's Great Society and War on Poverty programs. The markets dried up rather rapidly when the Johnson Administration was succeeded by the Nixon Administration. During the years of the energy shortages, there came into existence a great many energy consultants. When the shortage of oil abated, the market for the services of those experts dissipated rapidly. The introduction of the desktop computer produced an enormous boom in computer consulting, and spun off many satellite industries and consulting specialties. The computer consultant of today does not do it all; he or she has some specialty within the general field of computer consulting. Timing is an imponderable and unpredictable element, one of several that make marketing at least as much art as science.

Sometimes the marketability of a service is affected by that of other services or products. Video cameras for individual consumer use got off to a rather slow start because their usefulness was only to those who owned videocassette recorders. But now, when VCRs are almost as commonplace as radios and televisions, video cameras are moving far more briskly, very much in evidence among tourists and sightseers everywhere, all but demolishing the market for the 8mm home movie camera that was so popular a few years ago. (In fact, some enterprising individuals have made a business of converting home movies into videotape cassettes.) So convenient is videotape that even the commercial moviemakers of Hollywood now shoot all their scenes with video cameras, as well as with film cameras, because they can then see the "rushes" or "dailies" (proofs) of the day's shooting immediately after shooting, while there is time to reshoot the scene at once.

Because all businesses today use computers, especially desktop computers, and virtually all use database management and spreadsheet programs, many consultants focus on and specialize in services related to these kinds of software. However, the rapidly accelerating growth of home-based small businesses has had its effects, too. Most small businesses do not need to have special software written for them or even to have off-the-shelf software adapted, but they do have computer-related needs. They do need consulting services to train clients in various kinds of software, to help clients install programs, and other services that do not require programming services. Computer consulting is therefore no longer necessarily based on programming services, as it once was.

All of this is further evidence that there are no new needs, but only new and better ways of satisfying old, basic needs. Still, marketability also depends on other factors, as already suggested, as the consequence of the interdependence of the items in a marketing plan.

There are thus many factors affecting marketability that are not under your control. However, there are factors affecting the marketability of your service that are at least partially under your control.

Consider this: In the early days of computers, General Electric, RCA, Philco, Honeywell, Control Data Corporation, and IBM were among the large companies building and selling mainframe computers, but IBM dominated the field easily. Was their computer better than the others? Probably not. Was it cheaper than the others? Almost surely not. Was it marketed more effectively? Definitely. For one thing, and a very important one, IBM service was peerless, and that is in itself a major marketing strategy. Few things can alienate a client more rapidly than unreliable and indifferent service, and the opposite is equally true.

Make It Marketable

Do not rely entirely on any set of rules or guidelines. Creative imagination and the courage to break with the past and try a new idea, even when that violates some widely accepted rules—a bit of gambling instinct, that is—are often the keys to great marketing successes. Simply put, successful marketing often requires courage, even boldness, which means risk-taking. Robert Townsend, heading up the Avis car rental firm, was a risk taker. Instead of screaming the superlative qualities of Avis, he advertised his acknowledgment that Avis was only number two in the car rental business, but he turned that into a giant asset by going on to say that as number two in the industry, Avis tries harder, gives better service, and is generally more concerned with the customer's needs.

Marketing strategies and methods can make a product or service more marketable. Gifted marketers can outsell their competitors even when both are selling the same items. In fact, quite often and perhaps more to the point, the gifted marketer can often sell what competitors are unable to sell. That is, under certain circumstances, marketing can make the otherwise unmarketable item a success.

REACHING YOUR MARKET

You worked at deciding where—who and what—your market is. But do you know how and have the means to reach it? It's of no importance to know what or who your ideal market is if you can't reach it. However, in this modern world there are many ways to reach most markets—to present your offer, get the order, and fulfill it. You must somehow make a presentation of your offer and proposition.

Most consultants come to rely on word of mouth—referrals—for much and often all their consulting contracts. These can be personal referrals by satisfied clients and they can include referrals resulting from other activities, such as networking. If you manage to make a good enough impression on others, you will get some surprising referrals: Total strangers who know you only by reputation will often refer and recommend you to others. Strangers can gain that impression of you from your advertising and promotion generally—any of the methods we shall be discussing here.

However, that spontaneous phenomenon of referral by satisfied clients and strangers takes time to develop, and in any case develops primarily as a result of more direct marketing and sales activity, as presented in Figure 7.2. They include advertising, public relations and publicity, networking, direct marketing, and referrals from brokers. Any and all of these are used to lead to sales directly and indirectly. Use Worksheet 7.1 to consider these methods for making sales to see which fit your situation best and should be used. Check off the items you think will work for you in marketing and intend to use. But consider the following discussions before making your choices.

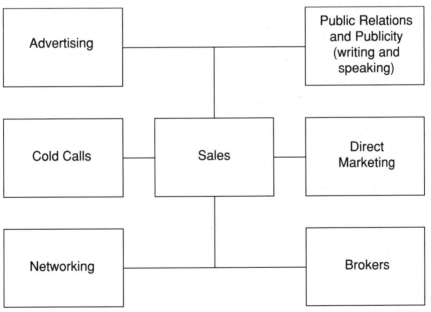

Figure 7.2.   Marketing and sales activities.

Worksheet 7.1.   Planning marketing tools and methods.

1. Routes to reach your target audience:

    ☐ Brokers
    ☐ Advertising
    ☐ Cold calls
    ☐ Networking
    ☐ Public relations and publicity
    ☐ Writing and speaking
    ☐ Direct marketing
    ☐ Other _____

2. Brokers:

    ☐ Brokers
    ☐ Job shops
    ☐ Other _____

3. Advertising:

    ☐ Print media
    ☐ Radio
    ☐ Special (for example, trade show, convention)
    ☐ Other _____

4. Cold calls:

    ☐ Personally
    ☐ Commission salesperson/finder
    ☐ Other _____

5. Networking:

    ☐ Formal
    ☐ Informal
    ☐ Other _____

4. Public relations and publicity:

    ☐ Press releases
    ☐ Newsletter publication
    ☐ Other _____

5. Writing and speaking:

    ☐ Journal articles
    ☐ Seminars
    ☐ Other _____

Worksheet 7.1. Continued.

6. Direct marketing:
   - ☐ Mailing campaign
   - ☐ Bids and proposals
   - ☐ Other _____

7. Other:
   - ☐ _____
   - ☐ _____
   - ☐ _____

Assignments via Brokers

Many consultants find it easier to do all their marketing via brokers and job shops. Economically, it makes sense. You will work for lower rates, probably, than you would command in direct billing to the client, but you are spared most of the cost of marketing, not only in out-of-pocket costs but also in the important matter of your time. That means less overhead time and more billable time, and so you may wind up better off financially, while you avoid the hassle of marketing and sales activity.

Theoretically, the broker is a prime contractor to the client, while you and others the broker places on the job—usually on the client's premises—are subcontractors. You bill the broker for your time on whatever basis you have negotiated and contracted.

Unfortunately, that arrangement is becoming a more and more uncertain proposition because the IRS today is highly skeptical of the consultant's status as an independent contractor where there is a third party acting as a labor contractor. The IRS is strongly inclined to view consultants working in this manner as temporary employees of the broker and insist that the broker act as an employer with regard to taxes. That denies the consultant the right to take ordinary deductions as overhead and other business expenses and makes the broker a job shop.

Many brokers are so intimidated by the IRS that they will not even attempt to qualify their operations as that of a prime contractor and subcontractors, but will only place consultants willing to work as temporaries. Many consultants who cannot somehow circumvent this object strongly enough so that they either flatly refuse to accept assignments via brokers or do so only when their need makes it unavoidable.

Advertising

Probably most beginning consultants consider media advertising as a means for winning clients. It seems the logical thing to do. Unfortunately, it is of limited value to most consultants because few clients turn to advertising in the media to find consultants. Still, it is not entirely without merit, and does work for at least some consultants. The Monday edition of the *Washington Post* includes a special tabloid as its business section, and consultants do advertise in two classified sections, titled Freelance Connection and Computer Services Directory, respectively. The first section carries any appeals from freelance writers, photographers, artists, paralegals, architects, accountants, and sundry other specialists. The latter section carries notices from computer programmers, suppliers, network engineers, and others. These notices clearly reflect something noted earlier, that the field has become so diversified that computer consulting today no longer revolves around programming services but offers ample opportunities for other relevant specialties.

In any case, media advertising is of limited usefulness for many, if not most, consultants. It probably would not be wise to place great reliance on it as a means for building your practice initially.

Cold Calls

Those who are not reluctant to go knocking on doors—making cold calls on business executives—tend to regard this direct marketing approach as the best one. There is some support for this idea if by

---

Advantages of Cold Calling

- You get to the decisionmaker and make your case directly and without delay.
- You get feedback immediately that tells you whether to persist, to follow up, or to go on to the next prospect.
- You get feedback that guides you in your presentation and tells you what services you should offer.
- Over the long haul, as experience accumulates, you learn early in the game what services sell best and are of greatest value to most prospects or, conversely, what kinds of prospects are most suitable to your needs and purposes.

"best" you mean most effective. Cold calling is, indeed, most effective and most efficient if it is done well—if you are aggressive, persistent, and coldly logical, and can wing it by being able to think on your feet and reacting spontaneously.

The advantages of cold calling as listed in the box at the top of the page give you a chance to make your consulting practice a one-call business to at least some extent because you may be able to capture some orders immediately, on the first call.

Cold calling is thus an excellent means, probably the best means, for gaining clients rapidly. Unfortunately, it is the least-favored method because it is the most distasteful kind of marketing for most of us. We shrink from approaching total strangers, especially on their own grounds, and we all but cringe in the anticipation (and realization) of rejection. Most of us thus tend strongly to turn to methods that are highly impersonal and shield us from direct, personal contact with strangers, especially when we are in the disadvantageous position of supplicants.

Networking

Networking is highly regarded as a means of finding clients via referrals. It is carried out both formally and informally. There are those entrepreneurs who organize special referral groups and meetings. These can vary from small groups meeting in someone's recreation room or private room of a local bar to the formal ballroom meeting, with cash bar, in a hotel. Either way, the idea is to bring together people from various environments who can refer business to each other. When networking, carry plenty of business cards and, as appropriate, small brochures to hand around, and keep moving, trying to have a few minutes' conversation and exchange of cards with everyone there. You may leave such a meeting with several referrals already in hand, and others in prospect.

On the other hand, there is informal networking that is far more popular, and perhaps more practical. It means belonging to associations and being active in them, attending meetings and conventions, serving on committees, and otherwise making yourself known to all and building a wide circle of acquaintances. Such activity raises your visibility and enhances your image, thus contributing to the generation of referrals.

Public Relations and Publicity

Mail order and *direct mail* are different terms to the purists, although most people use the terms interchangeably. *Public relations* is technically not the same thing as *publicity* but many people also use those terms interchangeably, although generally shortening it to PR. In these cases, the distinctions are relatively fine ones. Therefore, where I use the term *mail order* I refer also to direct mail, and when I refer to PR or public relations I refer also to publicity.

PR leads to referrals, just as those other methods do because they raise your image—if the image raised is a favorable one. Fortunately, some of the methods you can use are in themselves almost accolades or, at least, recognition of a high degree of professionalism. Having articles published in trade journals, for example, generally commands respect, and having a book published commands even more respect. When the training director of International Telephone & Telegraph went looking for someone to lead a marketing seminar, he found one of my books in the McGraw-Hill bookstore in New York and invited me to submit a proposal, which resulted in two contracts with the company.

The most-used tool of PR is the press release, a sample of which is shown as Figure 7.3. These are much underused by independent practitioners, either because they hate to write, as so many individuals do, or they can't think of anything to write about. It's not really that difficult to find topics for a press release. There is a logical order to the process:

1. Determine who you wish to reach with the release.
2. Decide what publications are read by these individuals.
3. Study sample copies of these publications.
4. Search for topics of interest.
5. Write and mail the release in as many copies as possible.

The release ought to be about consulting or your special field, of course. Building my image as a proposal specialist and government contracting consultant, I developed releases about the field. Several used anecdotes about novel government procurements as leads: The government renting mules and handlers, contracting to have the wild burros of the Grand Canyon rounded up, hiring a dramatic company to stage a colonial scene in an historical house at Yorktown, Virginia, and other such items. Each release went on to mention my service. But I could also use ordinary, dull facts by dramatizing them. I might report "270,000 Government Contracts to Small Business," or "Retail Furniture Stores Sell to the Government."

All it takes is a bit of imagination, and you can find items of interest everywhere—or take ordinary items and make them interesting.

Many independent practitioners find a simple newsletter a great PR tool. It need not be an elaborate publication. In fact, it can be a single sheet, printed on both sides, and does not have to have a regular schedule, but can be published every month or two, as you see fit or find the time.

PRESS RELEASE

NATIONAL ASSOCIATION OF TEMPORARY SERVICES
119 SOUTH SAINT ASAPH ST., ALEXANDRIA, VA. 22314

TELEPHONE: 703/549-6287   **FOR RELEASE:**
CONTACT: Bruce Steinberg   September 7, 1993

Temporary Help Services Industry Launches
its own version of the North American Free Trade Agreement (Nafta)

(September 7, 1993, Alexandria, VA) -- While politicians in
Washington jockey for position for the next showdown between the
Clinton Administration and Congress, two national trade
associations are implementing their own version of Nafta.

The National Association of Temporary Services (NATS), which
represents the temporary help industry in the U.S., and the
Federation of Temporary Help Services (FTHS), comprised of
Canadian temporary help companies, will conduct a joint
convention in Toronto from October 13, 1993, to October 16, 1993.

According to Samuel R. Sacco, executive vice president of
NATS, NATS represents more than 1,000 temporary help companies
operating over 8,300 offices in all 50 states and represents 85%
of U.S. temporary help industry sales. In 1992, the industry had
revenues of $25 billion (US). Figures for Canada are not known.

The four-day confab, held at The Westin Harbour Castle in
Toronto, will be the largest gathering of temporary help company
executives in North America. More than 1,400 attendees are
expected.

Each association will conduct its own separate annual
meeting as well as an award luncheon. However, all other
programs, workshops, and exhibitions at the convention, which is
being billed as "A Northern Classic," will be open to all
attendees. The speakers and workshop leaders will be a
combination of well-known American and Canadian business
professionals.
                         - more -

Figure 7.3.   Sample press release.

Writing and Speaking

Aside from releases—and you should certainly be sending these out as often as possible to as many relevant journals, newsletters, and other publications as possible—there are other kinds of special activity that will bring you inquiries and referrals. I refer here to writing and speaking. Both are extremely useful for making you more visible and more respected, which will seed referrals and inquiries.

Write articles for the periodicals of associations to which you belong, and also write articles for trade journals or professional journals and newsletters. If you are a real estate appraiser, write articles about what you do. Explain what appraisal is, what appraisers look for, how to maximize the appraisal on a property you are trying to sell. If you are an engineer, write about what is new in engineering, and what it means to engineers and users of engineering skills. If you are a training consultant, write about the latest publications, the latest tests, and the latest research findings in the field.

There is also public speaking. Perhaps you fear the platform. You are in good company; it's a most common fear. Work at overcoming it. Join committees in your associations and make verbal reports on your feet to warm yourself to the idea. Sit on panels addressing groups. Join groups that help you learn to speak publicly—Toastmasters, for example. Be a guest at others' seminars and, eventually, organize and present your own.

Direct Marketing

Sending out press releases is a form of direct marketing, a term that means seeking out prospective clients and pursuing them, rather than trying to induce them to call you as a result of a referral of some sort. Doing it by mail—using direct mail, that is—is one way that is relevant here.

Consulting is not a mail order business, at least not normally. That is, you can not normally package your consulting—a custom, personal service—and mail it to a client. (There are exceptions, but we will get to them later.) However, you can use direct mail to pursue and win clients. You can send out brochures and dignified sales letters. These may or may not bring back inquiries and referrals directly, especially not the first time you make a mailing, but the effect is cumulative: Eventually, if you keep sending out the mail, recipients will begin to respond, and the response will gather momentum. One point, however: This is effective only if you mail repeatedly to the same list of names and addresses. Mailing 1,000 pieces five times to the same 1,000 people will produce much better results than mailing 5,000 pieces once to 5,000 people. Learn the rudiments of this or contract with someone to do this for you. There are plenty of consultants in that field too.

Another form of direct marketing is submitting bids and proposals, especially the latter. Learn to write effective proposals or engage the services of someone who can do so. It may be the same person who does other copy and direct mail for you, but get someone good.

Other Marketing Ideas

You may have a number of other ideas for marketing tools, methods, and strategies. Space is provided for these in Worksheet 7.1, although there is an ample number of ideas for you to think about.

NEXT, THE "HOW TO"

Of course, you will not check off all the items in Worksheet 7.1. You may have some firm objections to writing or speaking—or perhaps both. That doesn't mean that you need abandon these tools. There are plenty of consultants around who can do this kind of work quite expertly. The idea here is to plan the methods for doing this work. The next chapter goes into the development of some of these materials, and you may want to preview that chapter quickly before you make final decisions about the items in Worksheet 7.1.

8

Planning the Presentations and Using the Tools

This is where "the rubber meets the road." Winning clients and making sales is the acid test of viability, and wishing won't make it happen: It requires planning and execution to do it well.

IT IS A MATTER OF PRESENTATION

Marketing is, in part at least, what you have been doing by working through the book thus far: Identifying your prospective clients, planning your accesses, and making your plans to go in pursuit of clients and sales. You have already made some decisions as to the marketing and sales methods you plan to use. You need also to plan the use of certain tools and materials to implement your marketing and sales plans. These are the tools you will use in gaining access to prospective clients, as you set those routes and goals in Worksheet 7.1.

To make a sale you must, of course, make a presentation to your prospective client. Don't be misled by that impressive word "presentation"; it is not necessarily a dog and pony show (although sometimes that is the way to go). It can be as simple as a fifty-word explanation of what you do and as complex as a formal lecture, with transparencies and printed handouts. You do, however, almost invariably need to make the most of that explanation and probably offer it in far more than fifty words to win each client for your consulting services. The size and nature of your presentations will vary enormously with the various circumstances—with the size of the job, the nature of the job, and the difficulty or complexity of the job, as well as with several more subtle factors.

For a brief preview, these are among the kinds of marketing and sales tools you are likely to need:

- Resumes
- Proposals
- Advertising copy
- Brochures
- Capability statements
- Releases
- Newsletters
- Seminar materials
- Sales letters

These are all presentation materials of one kind or another. Some of them are suitable to or useful for only certain sales situations, while others are almost universally useful and can be employed in all or almost all sales situations. But before we get into applications situations, much less the actual development of specific sales tools, let us have a brief look at some of the most basic and important sales principles.

WHAT MOTIVATES A PROSPECT
TO BECOME A CLIENT?

With the foregoing considerations, if it is not already apparent now, it is time to understand the basic nature of motivation: Motivation is an emotional factor, not a rational one. The sales argument that tries logically and objectively to prove the superior quality and performance of the product has its place in the sales presentation and in motivating the customer. But it is a decidedly secondary place and secondary consideration—almost a minor one—in bringing the prospect to a buying decision. That is because most of our decisions are based in emotional reactions, despite our efforts to conceal this elemental truth from ourselves. Most of us wish to believe that we are thoroughly rational and reasonable creatures, motivated by logic. Unfortunately that is not the case, or at least is only rarely the case. We are only partially rational, and are motivated far more by our emotions than by reason. However, our human egos reject the notion of irrational motivation, and so we insist on rationalizing our decisions and persuading ourselves that the irrational and often unwise emotional decisions we make are logical ones. That is the basis—the premise and the rationale—for my own theory of marketing, which has worked well for me and which I shall impart to you here. It is based on a quite simple basis of two elements of persuasion, elements I label "proof" and "promise." But to understand that concept fully, let's return for a moment to the premise that people do not buy things, they buy what these things do for them.

Many people entering the sales field are introduced to the acronym AIDA, which is intended to explain selling and advertising as the process and product of four ingredients (see the box below).

But does AIDA really explain motivation and sales success? I have always found this a rather strained effort to force-fit the elements into that mnemonic device, AIDA. I do not deny that the four elements are worthy objectives in every sales and advertising effort, but they are tentative and rather ill-defined swipes at defining and identifying the forces of selling, rather than true breakthroughs of analysis

---

A	[get] Attention
I	[arouse] Interest
D	[generate] Desire
A	[ask for] Action

and explanation. In fact, they raise more questions than answers about the process, to wit:

- Does it matter how one gets attention? Is any kind of or means for getting attention satisfactory to answer that first requirement or must it be some special kind of attention-getting device?
- Just how does one go about arousing interest? Is there not something a bit more to be said here on that subject, something a bit more helpful than merely the injunction to do it?
- As for generating desire, is that different from arousing interest? Or was that thrown in here to help form the acronym, which just happens—by coincidence, of course—to be also the title of a well-known Puccini opera?
- Finally, what is this "action" called for? The intention is to translate this into asking for the order, although nowhere have I found a dictionary that finds *action* to be a synonym of *order* or *sale.* This is probably an extreme case of force-fitting a term to create an acronym, one reason I have a distaste for most acronyms.

Aside from those shortcomings, my quarrel with AIDA is more fundamental: It suggests *what* you ought to do to achieve a sale, but is rather mute on the subject of *how* to go about this—how to get attention, how to arouse interest, how to generate desire. This renders AIDA considerably less than helpful. We ought to be able to improve on that.

Proof and Promise

In place of AIDA I offer a simpler form that is, I believe, considerably more definitive: proof and promise. It, too, requires an explanation that will be an abbreviated one here because extended discussion is beyond the intended scope of this book, but the principle is simple enough to explain quickly.

People do not buy things; they buy what the things do. As one astute observer put it, people do not buy quarter-inch drills; they buy quarter-inch holes. That, however, could be put into even more cogent and more useful terms: People buy do-it-yourself savings. People buy do-it-yourself satisfaction. People buy ego gratification. Even if it takes a $100 expenditure to do a $50 job, many people will make the expenditure because, for them, there are motivations greater than that of saving money. Understand, then, the true motivation is rarely to own the thing; it is to enjoy what the thing does—or what it helps you avoid, as in the case of insurance and alarms.

It is more or less taken for granted in business that the thing you offer to sell and the price you ask for it becomes known and referred to as "the offer." I quarrel with that. To me, the offer is the benefit I promise—to be happier, to be more attractive, to find greater convenience, to save money, to be protected from disaster, or other such boon.

What many refer to as the offer I prefer to call "the proposition." That is a statement of how one may take advantage of my offer and gain the benefit promised. It may as simple as stating the price, but may include other elements, depending on the individual case, such as terms for payment, credit cards acceptance, guarantees, delivery, free trial period, and other such matters.

The Promise

By now it may have occurred to you that since people are generally motivated by the promised benefit that will result from the purchase, what they are really buying is the promise. Yes, that *is* what they buy. They buy a promise to make them thin and happy, more secure, more attractive, richer, and, probably most frequently for those of us in the consulting field, free of a worrisome problem.

Is this what the customer is buying, then—a better figure, a more healthful physique, a better self-image? No, even that is not what the customer is buying, for you can't deliver that across the counter or through the mail. You can't deliver that at the point of sale no matter where or what that point of sale is, in fact; you can deliver at the point of sale only a product or service that, you say, will produce that benefit as a result of the customer's purchase and use of what you sell. So what the customer is really buying is the *hope* of one or more of those results. That is, the customer is really buying your *promise*, implicit or explicit, of those results. Hence, the concept that because you are really selling promises, the chief motivator in any sales effort is the promise of some result, even if the promise is to deliver something that is implied, rather than stipulated.

The Proof

The promise, if attractive enough, will command attention, arouse interest, and even generate temptation to buy without further ado. The greater the promised benefit, the more tempting it is. However, most clients are not naive. They will want more than allegations before they accept your promise, and the greater the promise, the more skeptical they will be and the more proof they will require before they accept your promise and believe in it. (Note: "Proof" is only a word, and in this case it means whatever the prospect will accept as proof or strong evidence. Once again, it is the prospect's *perception* that is decisive.)

This variability in the degree of proof required is true in some proportion to the cost of what you are selling, as well as being in some proportion to the magnitude of what you promise. Not surprisingly, the higher the cost, the greater the amount of proof required.

There are many kinds of proof you can furnish—testimonials, logical argument, authoritative statements, guarantees, certifications, and others; whatever the prospective client finds credible and will accept.

These considerations are of critical importance in marketing. Making sales, the ultimate goal of marketing, is an act of persuasion, and designing the offer and proposition is the blueprint for that act of persuasion. To get a swift education in this, study the advertising in newspapers, magazines, and on radio and TV to see where these elements are present.

USING YOUR SALES TOOLS

In the previous chapter, you worked out a list of the access routes you planned to pursue to reach prospective clients. Here, again, is the basic list you worked from:

- Brokers
- Advertising
- Cold calls
- Networking
- Public relations and publicity
- Writing and speaking
- Direct marketing
- Other

Let's take a look at Worksheet 8.1 while you consider the presentation needs for each of these situations and routes of approach to prospective clients. As you work your way through the following discussions, check off the appropriate items in the worksheet. These are the things you will plan to develop to implement your marketing plan.

Brokers

Of these categories, probably brokers, which includes job shops, are the easiest and least expensive markets to pursue, in terms of sales materials required, as well as of effort. (This is especially true for the technical specialties.) Job shops are firms that hire you for the sole purpose of selling your services as temporary employees of the job shops' clients. Your value to the job shop depends entirely on your acceptability to their client. Ergo, the job shop requires only your resume in a form and with content the client will accept. (Job shops generally submit resumes to their clients, who usually want to interview those whose resumes they accept.)

In theory, the situation with a broker is somewhat different, at least technically. In theory, the broker has a contract to supply cer-

Worksheet 8.1. Planning your sales tools.

1. Resume:
   - ☐ Single, all-inclusive
   - ☐ Multiple, for various applications
   - ☐ Database for spontaneous resume generation as needed
   - ☐ Proposals
   - ☐ Capability statements

2. Advertising:
   - ☐ Periodicals, classified
   - ☐ Periodicals, display
     - ☐ Pubset
     - ☐ Camera ready
     - ☐ "Homegrown"
     - ☐ Professional
   - ☐ Radio
     - ☐ Spot announcement
     - ☐ "Homegrown"
     - ☐ Professional
   - ☐ TV
     - ☐ Tape
   - ☐ Database

3. Cold calls:
   - ☐ Brochure
   - ☐ Capability statement
   - ☐ Script
   - ☐ Other leave-behinds
     - ☐ Calendar
     - ☐ Memo pad
     - ☐ Rolodex insert
     - ☐ Pens
     - ☐ _____

4. List of brokers:

   _____

   _____

   _____

Worksheet 8.1.   Continued.

5. Networking:
   - ☐ Formal
     - ☐ Plans to initiate
       - ☐ List of sites
       - ☐ Mailing list of prospects to invite
       - ☐ Cards and brochures
       - ☐ Announcements and invitations
       - ☐ Pens, calendars, and so on
     - ☐ List of others' organized network meetings
   - ☐ Informal
     - ☐ Database of organizations and events
       - ☐ Professional/trade associations
       - ☐ Conventions and seminars
       - ☐ _____
     - ☐ Cards, brochures, pens, calendars

6. Public relations and publicity:
   - ☐ Press releases
   - ☐ Newsletter
   - ☐ _____

7. Writing and speaking:
   - ☐ Articles for publication
     - ☐ For periodicals
       - ☐ Newspaper
       - ☐ Newsletters (others')
       - ☐ Association journals
     - ☐ Scientific/professional papers
   - ☐ Speeches
   - ☐ Seminars

8. Direct marketing:
   - ☐ Sales letter   ☐ Brochure   ☐ Response device   ☐ Return envelope

9. Other:

   _____

   _____

   _____

tain skilled people, and you negotiate a subcontract with the broker, which you normally execute by working on his client's site. To do this, you supply the broker with a proposal, usually a rather brief and informal one, and with your resume or its equivalent.

In practice today, the IRS has made it difficult to operate in this manner because they are insistent that self-employed individuals working through brokers are really temporary employees and not subcontractors. This has forced many brokers to operate as job shops.

If you opt to use brokers and job shops as important elements in your marketing, you will have to decide whether you can manage with one resume that sums up all your capabilities and credentials; with several resumes, each highlighting and focusing on a different area of strength; or a general database of personal information from which you will generate and tailor a resume for each case as it arises. All are viable alternatives, and all have been and are used by those consultants who work primarily for brokers and job shops.

Decide now whether you can manage well with one resume, need more than one, or need to build a database from which you can pull resumes tailored as necessary. (You can probably design a report format to generate individual resumes with minimal effort, and it might be a good idea to consider this in selecting DBM software.)

You need one other tool: You should do the research necessary to compile a list of brokers most suitable to your needs and to your desires. Ask around among friends and inquire in the associations to which you belong. Build a database of brokers, indicating their specialties and other significant factors.

Contracting and Subcontracting

If you work with brokers, even in the mode of subcontracting to them and working on the client's site, you are technically a subcontractor but actually working largely as a technical/professional temporary. As such, the broker is more interested in your personal resume detailing your skills and experience than in any ideas you have about how to approach the client's technical problems and solve or satisfy them. On the other hand, you may find some excellent business opportunities subcontracting with technical services firms and contracting directly with clients to handle parts of or all of complete projects. To pursue this mode of operation, you will need to develop *capability statements* and *proposals.*

A capability statement or capability brochure, as it is also referred to, is used generally to qualify as a bidder or proposer for a project. Clients often issue invitations to submit capability statements to develop a bidder's list—those deemed qualified to do the job and therefore invited to bid or submit a proposal.

Ordinarily, unless you are a large organization of diverse capabilities, you can standardize your capability statement and use it as a general introduction of your services to prospective clients. Thus, you need only one capability statement, which you can reproduce in some quantity.

Proposals, on the other hand, are custom presentations, written to offer the client your analysis of the client's problem/need/requirement, and explaining how you would solve the problem and what it would cost. For large jobs, that could mean a fairly substantial document. Portions of the proposal might be boilerplate and used over and over, but the proposal is normally tailored to and written especially for a given need and stated requirement. That is true whether you are submitting it to a client as the prime contractor or to a prime contractor as a subcontractor.

If you propose to do business in this manner—bid to undertake comprehensive projects—it is essential that you develop a proposal-writing capability and the resources needed for effective proposal writing.

Advertising

It is generally agreed among experienced consultants that conventional advertising via the media—print and broadcast—is rarely effective in winning clients and assignments for them, although there are exceptions. There are also those consultants who believe that they must somehow announce their presence in the media, at least in opening their new independent practice. This approach is entirely valid and important in those cases where the consultant is well known in the relevant industry. If this is the case with you, you may do well to use the print media to announce that you are entering private practice as an independent consultant.

The media referred to here are primarily the print media, periodicals, and the broadcast media, radio and TV stations.

All media advertising is expensive. Even small classified advertisements today run to several dollars per word in any periodical with large circulation. Such marketing is usually not fruitful as a direct means of winning clients, and I recommend great caution in relying on this as a chief marketing method.

You will need copy for print advertising, preferably camera-ready copy. Unfortunately, to buy "pubset" copy (copy set in type by the publisher) is often unsatisfactory, unless you can specify the copy and type requirements in detail. You will probably do well to have a professional copywriter—for example, a local advertising agency or advertising consultant/copywriter—handle it all for you.

If you use TV, you will have to have a tape produced. Again, you can use an advertising agency or you can find a freelance specialist who handles this kind of work.

As in the case of marketing via brokers, if you are going to use media advertising, you should build a list, at the least, and preferably a database, of periodicals and broadcasters most suitable to your needs—those reaching the prospects you want to reach.

Cold Calls

Distasteful though it is to most of us, making cold calls is probably the least expensive and most effective marketing approach open to us. You can do this kind of calling by telephone, as well as in person, but the personal call is the best. You will get plenty of rejections—executives who won't see you or who will be courteous but uninterested—but you need to strike oil only occasionally—perhaps once or twice a month, if you win substantial projects—to make the effort worthwhile.

You will need business cards, of course, and some kind of brochure. You will find it worthwhile to have a good capability statement to leave with those prospects you meet who appear to be interested. You may also find it worthwhile to leave other items that help you create and maintain a good level of visibility.

Be sure, also, to have a notepad with you to make notes, when you do find an interested prospect. You will want to follow up, in such cases, by making a subsequent appointment to make a full presentation or to offer a proposal. You rarely close a sale on the initial call—consulting is ordinarily not a one-call business—so you must plan to arrange the follow-up. Never leave a meeting with an even mildly interested prospect without planning and arranging some specific and definite follow-up with the prospect.

Networking

Networking can be formal or informal. Whichever it is, be sure you are equipped with cards, brochures, and a notepad of some sort for taking notes. You can also give out advertising novelties—pens, calendars, and so on—if you wish when networking. It all helps raise your visibility, a most important part of all marketing.

Public Relations and Publicity

We touched on press releases previously as one of the major tools of PR and publicity. Plan to issue these as often as possible, if you wish to pursue PR for the benefits it can bring you at little cost. A newsletter is another great tool of PR, and is worth considering seriously. It does not have to be a glossy affair; simple newsletters work well also. It can be a quarterly or even without a defined frequency so that the burden of pressing deadlines is relieved: Some people publish newsletters on no schedule at all, but only as they perceive a need for a new edition, have some new information they wish to impart, or have some spare time to devote to the task. Actually, much of what is to follow and some of what has already been presented here can be deemed to be part of PR and publicity activities. Writing for publication and public speaking certainly fit that description.

Writing and Public Speaking

You may be among the many people who shrink from writing and retreat even more from public speaking. If so, that is a misfortune, for those are two valuable activities for everyone—especially for consultants. Writing for publication in respectable journals and, especially, writing books are rewarding writing activities in more than one way. It does enhance your professional image, as well as elevate your visibility, of course, and almost automatically produces at least occasional inquiries that turn into consulting jobs. Public speaking also has that salutary effect on your professional image and reputation.

If you work at it, you can get yourself invited to speak on radio and TV talk shows, especially the call-in variety. Talk show hosts welcome such participation. Find some interesting aspect of your work and tell the talk show's producer (not the host) about it. The producers generally make all the arrangements for guests, although the host may suggest candidates to the producer. In many cases, you can be a guest while seated comfortably at your own desk, telephone in hand.

If you are reluctant to write and speak because of distaste for or fear of these activities, perhaps you can condition yourself in stages to these, as many others have done. Write brief articles for the journals and brief papers for professional symposia and proceedings—even letters to the editor. Write and present your own papers at these gatherings of your peers. Sit on panels with others, and be a guest speaker at others' seminars for brief presentations—perhaps as little as ten or fifteen minutes. These experiences will help you overcome platform fever, and even develop a taste for the platform, if you are like most of us. You will come to enjoy being the center of attention for a short while and earning applause. Get deeply involved in the affairs of associations to which you belong—a local Lion's club or Rotary club, for example.

Direct Marketing

Direct marketing by mail is the chief manifestation of that which is referred to as *direct response marketing*. It is also almost synonymous with that which is referred to as *mail order*. The differences that distinguish direct mail from mail order are not especially significant, and are of interest primarily to purists. It would probably be most accurate to say that mail order includes direct mail as one way of doing business by mail.

It is not easy to sell consulting services by mail. You can sell your services in the form of a newsletter and reports covering the general case—for example, how to organize a database management file or write a batch file—but that is not the sole extent of what direct mail can do for you. You can't deliver your basic consulting service by mail, of course, but you can do much of your prospecting and selling by mail, so it is a valid marketing medium even for consulting services.

The basic direct mail package includes a minimum of three obligatory items: a sales letter, a brochure, and a "response device." The latter can be an order form, a request for more information, or an invitation to call and make an appointment to discuss what you wish to offer—that is, to make a personal presentation. However, equally important—even more important in the opinions of many direct mail professionals—is the quality of the mailing lists.

Mailing Lists

Mailing lists are an essential of direct mail, and probably the most difficult part of launching a direct mail marketing campaign is getting the right mailing lists. There are a great many list brokers, firms who rent lists of names and addresses to those who market by mail; they are quite easy to find. They are brokers because, with only occasional exceptions; they rent mailing lists owned by others, earning commissions on the list rentals.

There are, generally speaking, two kinds of lists: response lists and compiled lists. Response lists are those names and addresses of people who have bought by mail or who have inquired by mail, and they are classified and value-rated according to those qualifiers. The names and addresses of those who have spent substantial sums recently in direct mail purchases or who buy regularly by mail are rated high in value. Those who can be certified only as having bought by mail some undefined time in the past have a lesser value. And those who have inquired by mail but cannot be certified to have ordered anything are rated even lower in value.

Mailing lists are sorted and classified in many ways—by what they buy, by how much they have spent, by demographics such as where they live and how they live, and by numerous other measures. The lists are of subscribers, of church-goers, of political donors, and sundry other distinguishing characteristics.

You don't buy these response lists; you rent them, and you must pay for each use, except for the names and addresses of those who buy from you or respond to your solicitation. ("Buying" does not have to be literal fact but includes responding in whatever way you have asked for a response.) The prospect then becomes your client and you can reuse that name and address, of course; it is now yours, and you have begun to build your own "house list."

Some list firms compile lists from various sources—directories of all kinds. You can virtually buy these lists. That is, once you pay for the first use, you can use them over and over. You don't own the lists, except for those who become your clients, so you can't resell or rent them, but you are free to use them over and over for repeat mailings.

Generally speaking, compiled lists are considered to be of lesser value than response lists. That may or may not be true for you and the application you make of whatever lists you use.

It is possible to compile your own lists, whereupon the lists are yours, of course. The important thing, however, is not that the list becomes yours or that it may cost you less out of pocket to compile your own; the important thing is that you have greater control and can be highly selective in your compilations. It's relatively easy to do so now, since we all have computers that will sort, merge, clean, manipulate, and manage the lists. In some cases, doing your own compiling is the only way to get the lists you want. When I wanted lists I had difficulty finding ready-made ones suitable for my needs (I wanted lists of government contractors), so I began to compile my own lists from newspaper advertisements (the help-wanted ads), from which I could easily infer the nature of the company doing the advertising. You can use this route too: The Sunday editions of some of the large daily newspapers are an excellent source of such information, as are the several special help-wanted tabloids published every week as compilations of the help-wanted advertising from those newspapers. You can often get copies of membership directories of associations, perhaps glean some of what you want from the yellow pages. Also, many communities and even state governments publish directories of businesses in their jurisdiction. Just this morning I picked up a copy of the latest edition—the 30th—of the *Community Guide to Wheaton-Kensington*, for example. (I was able to get several lists of government contractors from the Small Business Administration and other federal agencies when I was doing my compilations.) I built lists of many thousands in this manner.

Sell Copy

Most of the items we have been discussing as marketing and sales tools represent what is referred to by many copywriters as sell copy. They are kinds of literature designed primarily to persuade prospects to become clients—to buy the service or product, and they include the three items that comprise a basic direct mail package. Some of them are direct sell, exhorting the reader to order the item or items immediately; others are indirect sell, supporting the direct sell pieces without including the direct exhortations to buy. These indirect sell pieces include such items as specification sheets and item descriptions.

Sales letters. The sales letter is probably the most common and most frequently used sales tool. It is used in several ways and in several situations, but there are three basic situations that call for its use. The direct-mail package is typically built around the sales letter, which introduces and explains the offer.

Brochures. The brochure reinforces whatever was said in the sales letter and follows the guidelines laid down for all sell copy. In this case, the sales effort is somewhat indirect, in that direct mail used here is primarily a prospecting device, seeking to evoke responses—generate sales leads—that you can follow up by telephone and in person.

Response devices. When selling some product by mail, the principal response device is an order form of some sort. In this case, you don't expect orders (unless you are selling some product that is ancillary to your consulting services); you seek responses that signal the interested prospect who is likely to become a client. Therefore, your response device in this case is a card or form that invites the respondent to send for a report, more information, or even a full-blown presentation (see Figure 8.1). According to your own situation, you can offer several suggestions as to why the prospect ought to hear what you have to say. For example, you should list several of the most common problems that people have vis-à-vis the service you offer. Were I doing this today, I would offer to reveal to them something of how to develop winning proposal strategies, find worry items, and create attention-getting proposals.

The response device may be a postcard or it may be a larger form with a response envelope. In either case, it is a good idea to have the response device preaddressed to you and postage free for the client's convenience, so it need merely be popped directly into the mail.

Office Organization Services, Inc.

333 17th Road, Suite 211
Smartsville, PA 18119
(215) 555-1112

☐ We are having difficulties with the following:
   ☐ our filing systems
   ☐ handling our correspondence
   ☐ meeting our schedules
   ☐ _____

I would like to discuss our needs with you.

☐ We are in need of general office reorganization and would like a general presentation to learn more of the services you can provide.

Please call me to make arrangements for your visit. I understand that I incur no obligation as a result of this request.

Name: _____

Tel: _____

Figure 8.1.   A response device.

9

Zeroing in on Your Market

Knowledge is power in marketing, as it is in other things. Perhaps it is even more so in marketing. Intelligence is the eyesight of marketing. Without it, you are flying blind; with it, you increase your win record manifold and you shorten the time to reach the level of self-sufficiency in marketing. There are a great many means available for gathering intelligence to support your marketing efforts but they need to be planned in advance.

MARKET RESEARCH VERSUS MARKET INTELLIGENCE

Earlier, you filled out worksheets in which you identified what you thought would be the main targets for your marketing, including the special segments or niches you anticipated. That was a good beginning, but only a beginning. In the business world, most major market targets are out in plain sight and so are rather obvious: Businesses advertise their goods and services, and you can easily infer what they normally have need for and are most likely to buy. Simple logic is all you need to do that. It is reasonable to assume that if you are a tax expert and offer your services as a consultant in matters of taxes, almost any company or other business organization is a possible prospect for your services. On the other hand, you know that accounting firms have great reliance on computers and computer software, and that at least some accounting firms will require expert services to support their operations—that is, are prospects for you if you are a computer consultant.

What you don't know and can't infer simply from knowing that such firms and such needs exist is which organizations need help in solving their tax problems, or which accounting firms need computer-related help, or exactly what kinds of problems they need help in solving. Market research will tell you or at least give you a basis for estimating how many accounting firms are in your service area, how much computer consulting service they buy, and what kinds of problems they need solved or what kinds of services they need performed. What that won't tell you is *which* accounting firms need help at any given time or just *what kind* of help they need. That knowledge is market *intelligence.* That is what you need to plan for also: How will you get the specific knowledge that will enable you to market efficiently, and perhaps completely avoid any necessity for cold calls?

The Inconspicuous Markets and Niches

This is not to overlook or ignore the fact that companies in the business world and other organizations often let the world know their needs by advertising and asking for bids and proposals for specific services and projects. In fact, there are various and sundry publications devoted to helping business people learn promptly about all bid opportunities in their field. There is the *Commerce Business Daily,* published by the federal government to announce needs and bid opportunities, along with notices of awards to prime contractors, for example. (The latter notices should serve as leads to possible subcontracts.) Maryland publishes its major needs and bid opportunities in its own *Maryland Register,* although most state and local governments use the classified advertising section of the local newspaper to publish notices under Bids & Proposals. The construction industry is served by McGraw-Hill's *Dodge Reports*, and many other industries in which contracting is a principal element of activity have their own special reports of bid and proposal opportunities. Much of the marketing information you need is available to you directly via these publications.

Developing and Maintaining an Awareness of Markets

Of course, not all market targets are obvious. Many organizations are inconspicuous, and you can hardly market effectively to organizations of whose very existence you are completely unaware. In many ways the biggest problem in selling to some markets, such as government agencies and many kinds of nonprofit organizations, is "finding the doors": learning where and how to uncover these markets and all the business opportunities they represent. That is what market intelligence means to me, in part. Yes, there is more. Learning of the specific requirements of possible clients is one kind of market intelligence. Learning of the existence of markets that are almost invisible is another one of the ways in which I distinguish market intelligence from market research. And specific bits of information that help you win contracts is yet another. Competitor intelligence— who your direct competitors are, how what they offer compares with what you offer, and how their methods of marketing compare with your own marketing methods—is still another important aspect of marketing intelligence.

GATHERING MARKET INTELLIGENCE

Now turn to Worksheet 9.1 to plan some of the basic ways you can gather market intelligence. If you are interested in marketing to government agencies, you will want to monitor their announced needs, and also file applications to be included on their various lists of bid-

Worksheet 9.1.   Gathering market intelligence.

1. Sources of market intelligence you will use:
    - ☐ *Commerce Business Daily*
        - ☐ Paper (printed) version   ☐ On line version
    - ☐ Daily newspapers
        - ☐ Business news
        - ☐ Classified advertisements (bids and proposals)
    - ☐ Special publications
        - ☐ *Dodge Reports*
        - ☐ _____
        - ☐ _____

    - ☐ File applications for inclusion on bidders' lists
        - ☐ Federal agencies
        - ☐ State and local agencies
        - ☐ Major organizations
    - ☐ Computer communication
        - ☐ Subscribe to major public databases
        - ☐ Monitor relevant BBS and relevant services
    - ☐ Special measures
        - ☐ Ask for and attend prebid/preproposal conferences
        - ☐ Attend public bid openings
        - ☐ Get debriefings where possible (for example, government markets)
        - ☐ _____

2. Maintain a marketing library:
    - ☐ Business directories
        - ☐ Publications of state/local chambers of commerce
        - ☐ General business directories
        - ☐ *Thomas Register*
        - ☐ *Standard & Poor's*
        - ☐ *Dun & Bradstreet*
        - ☐ *National Directory of Names & Addresses*
        - ☐ _____

    - ☐ Competitor information
        - ☐ Competitors' brochures
        - ☐ Competitors' proposals
        - ☐ Competitors' contracts (information about)
        - ☐ Other information about competitors
        - ☐ _____

Worksheet 9.1.   Continued.

3. Build marketing databases:
    - ☐ Client lists
      - ☐ Current and past clients
        - ☐ General information on client
        - ☐ Types of past contracts
        - ☐ Names and positions of key individuals
        - ☐ News of
        - ☐ Construct profiles
        - ☐ _____

    - ☐ Prospect lists
      - ☐ General information (descriptive)
      - ☐ Type of services bought from others
      - ☐ Past efforts to sell to
      - ☐ News of
      - ☐ _____

    - ☐ Gathering the information for the marketing databases
      - ☐ Personal observation
      - ☐ Mail/telephone sales calls and surveys
      - ☐ Trade news
      - ☐ Organization's own literature
      - ☐ _____

4. Subscribe to public databases and other online services:
    - ☐ CompuServe   ☐ GEnie   ☐ SBA   ☐ NTIS
      - ☐ _____
      - ☐ _____

5. Attend/participate in various activities:
    - ☐ Conventions
      - ☐ Your own industry/associations
      - ☐ Industries/associations of potential clients
      - ☐ Related industries/associations
    - ☐ Symposia and conferences
      - ☐ Your own industry/associations
      - ☐ Industries/associations of potential clients
      - ☐ Related industries/associations
    - ☐ Trade shows
      - ☐ Your own industry/associations
      - ☐ Industries/associations of potential clients
      - ☐ Related industries/associations

    - ☐ _____

ders. However, be aware that many other large organizations maintain lists of bidders, and it may be in your interest to request your inclusion on as many of those lists as possible.

A Marketing Library

One of the things you should do is set up and maintain a marketing library. Aside from general books and periodicals of interest, there are a number of specific directories that are helpful in identifying organizations and individuals in those organizations. A few are listed in the worksheet, with space provided to add others of your choice. There are also the publications of local industries and businesses published by local chambers of commerce and business clubs, as mentioned in Chapter 5.

Electronic Avenues of Intelligence

There are a great many online services available today. There are electronic bulletin board systems (BBS), some run as a hobby, others run as a medium for the members of a group, some as a marketing tool by business firms, and some as a service by government agencies of various sorts. For example, a great many public library systems today have BBS via which a caller can browse through the library's catalog and determine which branch has any given book on its shelves at the moment. Utility services, such as CompuServe and others, have conferences or forums for various specialists and serving various interests, including consulting. Public databases offer an almost unimaginable array of information to which they can provide access. Here are just a few categories that may prove useful in your marketing efforts:

Summaries of civil suits and court decisions
Chemical sciences and engineering data

Scientific and engineering news items
Accounting and economics
Socioeconomic data
Banking information
Construction industry news and reports
Press releases of major corporations and government agencies

Your Own Marketing Databases

The notion of databased marketing has been taking hold recently, especially in the direct marketing fraternity. The basic concept is to build a database of your clients in which you record individual data about each client so that when you wish to make an offer—perhaps to conduct a direct mail campaign—you can target your prospects quite closely. For example, if you know local area networks, which means tying together all the computers in an organization so that they are a system, your prospective clients are going to be only those who have two or more computers. It would be wasteful of your time and money to solicit prospects who have only one computer. Perhaps you find that only organizations with five or more computers are good candidates for your service. Your marketing database should contain information to enable you to select a list of clients with five or more computers.

This philosophy should be extended to include a marketing database of prospective clients, although it may be more difficult to get the individual information about each prospect. With clients, you have the opportunity to learn something of the client's organization, operations, resources, and needs via your direct contact in providing services to the client. You also have ready access to the client's brochures, annual reports, and other literature. With prospective clients, your access is much more limited, although you do have the possibility of gathering the prospect's literature, reading information in the trade press, and making sales calls (in person or by telephone) in which you make it a point to gather as much information as possible for your databases.

Attend or Participate in Conventions and Trade Shows

Almost every industry and most associations of any size have annual conventions and trade shows, often as combined events. Many of these are golden opportunities to gain valuable information. You have the opportunity to gather the literature of, attend presentations by, and chat with both competitors and prospective clients.

These events—most held annually—present opportunities of more than one kind. They do present many opportunities to gather market intelligence to add to the building of your marketing databases, but there are a number of other benefits to be gained if you take full advantage of these events, all connected directly and indirectly with marketing—with winning clients and contracts.

Obviously, you cannot attend all the events of interest and still have enough time to devote to income-producing work. You must choose among the many events. There are three main criteria, as indicated in the worksheet under each category of event: The events sponsored and presented by your own industry or profession, those of industries and professions of potential clients, and those that are related somehow to your work.

There are three major objectives (and criteria for choosing the events) you should address in participating in these events:

1. Make contacts and establish sales leads for direct marketing purposes. Gather as much information as you can on prospective clients. Educate yourself steadily in identifying best prospects and learning what they need and what they find most appealing in selecting consultants as contractors. This is a byproduct, but that does not make it a less valuable benefit or a less important criterion in your selections. Finding clients and contracts ought to be your primary goal. The principal criterion in deciding to which events you will allocate your time ought to be which are most likely to help you directly in winning clients and closing sales.

2. Learn as much as you can about your competitors, as suggested earlier: who and what they are, how they compare, and what it is likely to take to hold your own against them. Gather information on them—read their literature. The ability to outshine your competitors is one of the keys to marketing success.

3. Use these occasions to polish your own professional image and to elevate your visibility. By participating actively, as in presenting a seminar or being a guest speaker at someone's seminar, you enhance your professional image. Equally important—probably more important, in fact—is making yourself known to as many people as possible. Some clients will find your offers more appealing because they have heard you speak or chatted with you at one of these events, but more often a client will be receptive simply because he or she knows who you are.

The fact is that most people will accept you as qualified in what you do without any proof, especially if you have become a familiar figure. Making yourself as widely known as possible, in connection with the kind of work you do as a consultant, is a most valuable marketing activity. The objective, however, must be to make yourself widely known to and among those you see as prospective clients. Don't make the common mistake of seeking to elevate your image among your peers (unless you seek subcontracts and associates); it's with clients you want to become well known.

Another point: With what activities ought you to be directly involved to further your purposes of becoming as well known and as well respected as possible? That is a subject that merits another worksheet, 9.2, to help you plan event activities.

In planning the activities in which you will engage in attending and participating in annual events, bear in mind the principle just enumerated: Remember who your targets are. You want to always address your activities to those who are the best prospects to become your clients. If you are an independent direct marketing consultant, for example, it is not likely that making yourself better known to other independent direct marketing consultants will help you win business. There are possible exceptions, of course, but it isn't productive to address yourself to the exceptions. Address yourself to that which is the general rule.

Here is where the usefulness of the earlier worksheets ought to become apparent: You need a clear view of whom you seek as pro-

Worksheet 9.2.   Planning your event activities.

1. General circulation (informal networking):
    - ☐ Meeting and chatting
    - ☐ Have available for handout
        - ☐ Cards and brochures
        - ☐ Copies of your newsletter
        - ☐ Advertising specialties
        - ☐ _____
    - ☐ Arranging follow-up
        - ☐ Lunches
        - ☐ Meetings
        - ☐ Presentations
        - ☐ _____
        - ☐ _____

2. Seminars/workshops:
    - ☐ Full day
    - ☐ Half-day
    - ☐ Less than half-day

3. Exhibit booth:
    - ☐ With audiovisual display
    - ☐ With advertising giveaway
    - ☐ With informal discussion
    - ☐ With copies of articles/books you have written
    - ☐ _____

4. Sideshow:
    - ☐ Sales room
        - ☐ With formal presentations
        - ☐ Without informal presentations/chats
    - ☐ Hospitality suite
        - ☐ With formal presentations
        - ☐ With informal presentations/chats
    - ☐ Cocktail party
    - ☐ _____

spective clients to decide which events to attend and how to participate most usefully in those events.

General Circulation/Networking

Many attendees do nothing special at the major annual events. They
think it sufficient to circulate freely, networking style, meet as many
people as possible, and hand out as many business cards and brochures as possible. They rely on statistical probability: If they maximize
the number of people they meet, greet, shake hands with, and hand
out cards and brochures to, they will get some percentage of return in
new clients and contracts. It is a marketing philosophy that works for
them. It depends on numbers—that is, meeting and chatting with
enough others and handing out enough cards and brochures to gain
the advantages of statistical probability. If you happen to be publishing
a newsletter, this is a good occasion to carry a supply with you and
hand out copies to everyone you meet. It is also an excellent occasion
to carry and distribute an advertising specialty, such as a pocket calendar, a memo pad, a card-size calculator, or other.

You do not have to confine yourself to normal networking objectives, however. Those are generally directed to winning referrals that
are likely to lead to contracts. You can and should set more concrete
objectives. Whenever you meet someone who represents a business
organization that seems "right" for what you do, try to set up preliminary arrangements to make a formal presentation to the other's executives, perhaps even offer a free one-hour seminar or workshop
that confers a benefit on the client, while it represents a sales presentation for you. It is poor marketing and sales practice to allow the
meetings with prospects to taper off into indecisive nothingness, with
vague statements like, "Let's do lunch sometime." That is almost always a waste of time. Try to end each meeting with someone who
appears to be a reasonably good prospect with a clear agenda for
follow up agreed to by both of you. Be prepared to do something of
this sort by having some relevant propositions clearly in mind.

Participating in annual events by general circulation or networking is a relatively passive way of participating in the event. Although it
has its own merits and does work satisfactorily for many individuals,
there are several more active and more aggressive ways of taking ad-

vantage of these annual gatherings, each of which offers the same benefits as general circulation and networking do, but are usually far more productive in creating actual sales opportunities and, eventually, new clients and new contracts.

Seminars and Workshops

Seminars are both major and popular elements in many of these annual events. These presentations are convenient avenues to exploiting the advantages of public speaking discussed earlier and listed as a topic in earlier worksheets. In participating in the convention of *Training* magazine, for example, I usually opted to conduct two or three of the three-hour seminars that were a major feature of that annual event.

No fees or honoraria were paid me for these seminars, but my expenses to New York (the convention site) and attendance at the convention were covered. I repeated this activity for several years, and enjoyed gaining several new clients and contracts as a result. Even if seminars are not a planned event, you may be able to propose a brief seminar or two to the sponsors of the event as a popular attraction.

Seminars do not have to be counted in days or half-days: It is possible to prepare brief seminars of an hour or two, and many would appreciate such brief seminars in preference to dedicating an entire day or half-day. Brief seminars provide an opportunity to make what amounts to a formal sales presentation, hand out literature, and provide samples of your skills and knowledge by responding to questions from attendees. You also have the opportunity to meet individually with attendees after the session is over, and I found that to be especially fruitful.

If the event does not make provision for seminars and the sponsors and managers of the event do not react well to your recommendation to offer them, all is not lost: There are alternatives.

Exhibit Booths

The most direct way of marketing your services at an annual event is by renting and operating a booth of your own in the exhibit hall. The direct purpose of the booth is to develop good sales leads, but the booth also provides an opportunity to firm up leads and even close sales on the spot. An exhibit booth will provide maximum exposure at the convention: All those attendees milling about and strolling up and down the aisles of the exhibits will pass your booth. You need to do something to cause the strollers to stop and see what it is you offer.

This is a case where an advertising novelty of some sort is almost mandatory. A key chain, calendar, poster, calculator, or other useful novelty will attract visitors and induce them to stop at your booth. Exhibitors with products to sell often offer samples of their products. You sell services as your primary business activity and possibly your only one. What you can offer passerbys to induce them to stop for a moment is literature and/or entertainment. You may have an audio-visual presentation, for example. Nowadays, most exhibitors use a TV and VCR with tape as the most efficient means of presenting an audiovisual. Of course, you may also have ancillary products—newsletters, books, and others—and may make those available to any who want them. And if you have written articles for the journals of your profession, by all means have reprints of these freely available. Also, if you have written a book and had it published, even if by some obscure small press, have copies available for display, at least.

However you organize your booth and its attractions, it is probably a good idea to have a small table and a few chairs at your booth for prospects to sit and chat with you about what you have to offer them as a consultant.

Sideshows

In trade shows and most professional or industrial conventions, there are exhibit halls, where the main show takes place: The major players in the profession or industry have their booths, with their exhibits, their literature, and their presentations. Around the fringes of the "big top" or "main tent" (there *is* a circus atmosphere to this spectacle) are the many sideshows, the smaller players on the edges or outskirts of the main event. Here, the "little guys" of the industry make their stand, offer their presentations, and make themselves known. But they are still part of the overall show, even if consigned to the fringes. And there is yet another layer to uncover.

In most convention centers and major hotels who host these annual events, there is a periphery of interested participants who are not entrants in the formal exhibits but are still interested enough to rent separate rooms adjacent to the exhibit hall to stage their own presence and presentations. Here, they may have a pure and simple sales presentation—a speaker on a dais armed with a pointer, a set of charts, and a microphone—or simply a room with coffee available, literature on display and a representative moving about to greet and get acquainted with visitors. Here, you can also do the things you would do with people you meet casually in networking, but since they are visitors, perhaps interested primarily in a cup of coffee and resting their feet at one of your tables or chairs, you have a greater opportunity to get acquainted and explore possibilities for follow-up activity.

There is a variation of this that carries the idea and the opportunities even further. It is the hospitality suite. The hospitality suite is generally a hotel suite, in the hotel where the convention is held or in a nearby hotel when the convention is in some other facility, such as a convention center. Guests are invited by distribution of invitations and posters at the convention. In the suite you offer literature, light refreshments, and presentations you think appropriate.

Obviously, to belabor the point a bit, you wish to attract prospective clients, and so you choose the events where the usual attendees are those prospective clients. Getting them to visit you in a separate suite of rooms gives you the advantage that there are no distracting competitive events immediately adjacent (although there may be a number of hospitality suites offered). You do have a much better grip on your prospects' attention in the environment of a hospitality suite.

Cocktail parties, being social events, are always popular at these annual events. Probably one-half the attendees of your cocktail party will be possible prospects, and that may be a generous estimate. But it is a fact: Cocktail parties attract everyone. Most of us enjoy parties, as well as the "happy hour" type of snacks served at such events. (Yes, food is very much a desirable feature of the cocktail party.)

I think it almost mandatory to have an ample number of tables and chairs available at these cocktail parties. Despite the fact that it is a social event, what is true for all the other events discussed is true here also: You can make business contacts and develop sales leads while enjoying yourself and others' company. Most of us need a table and chair to sit and have serious business discussions.

10

Rates and Pricing

THE BASIC VARIABLES

Among the most frequently expressed concerns, uncertainties, and questions of those new to consulting is that of pricing their services. That means, in most cases, setting their fees. Confusion exists concerning both rates and the basis for those rates.

Surprisingly enough, many consultants who have been practicing for a considerable length of time have not yet reached firm conclusions in these matters, and are still groping for more light on the subject of what they can and should charge for what they do. They are as fearful of charging too much as they are reluctant to charge too little.

As is the case with many other matters, there are no absolutes or standards. Typically, consultants charge fees based on time periods, usually as an hourly or daily rate. Aside from this, there are a great many variables that fall into several classes:

- The nature of your work and typical length of assignment.
- The market for what you do, including the common practices of others in your field and the economy, local or otherwise.
- Your own goals and business philosophy.

That isn't all of it by any means. Each of these broad categories of variance encompasses several elements that are, in turn, also variables. Thus, the matter of setting rates may be a simple one for some consultants, who appear to have an instinct directing their choices, but it is a matter of serious analysis for many who do not have an instinctual feeling for what they ought to require of clients.

The Nature of Your Work

Consultant services vary widely; some types of consulting tend to lengthy assignments, while others are characterized by quite brief assignments. For some consultants, their typical assignment is a project of weeks' and even months' duration, while for others their typical assignment is for a few days, at most. Also, for some consultants, a typical assignment occupies their full time until it is completed, while for others a typical assignment requires periods of effort with gaps between them.

A security consultant might be called on for a few hours to review the physical security of a plant and make a general report, for example. In my own consulting work as a proposal specialist, a typical assignment required my full time and attention for a period of some days, rarely much more than a week. An engineering consultant might be needed for several months. One associate of my own spent months in Kuwait after the Gulf War, along with many other consulting engineers and oil-field specialists.

Of course, these are not constants. On occasion, I have been asked to provide only a few hours of my time to help a client analyze a requirement or identify a strategy, and occasionally I have had assignments of longer term than usual. We all are subject to nonroutine assignments. However, by the nature of what we do as our specialties, our typical assignments can be any of those listed in the first item of Worksheet 10.1.

You will have to determine which of the descriptions in the worksheet is most applicable to your own case, as a first consideration. It would hardly be practicable to charge a daily rate if your typical assignments are counted in hours, rather than in days, so an hourly rate is more appropriate in such a case. On the other hand, if your typical assignment is a long-term project with clearly defined requirements, you may find it best to work on a "for the job" fixed price. Or, in some cases, clients may wish to work that way, rather than on the basis of a time-based fee or rate.

The Market for What You Do

There is such a thing as "a market" for most things—the average prices that clients are accustomed to and, probably, willing to pay for whatever services you provide. What most of your direct competitors charge and the economy, general and local, are both factors. If your practice is primarily local, it is the local economy and the local competition that set the market. If you practice on a national scale, it is the national economy and competition you must consider in determining what the market is. And if your practice or intended practice is an international one, you must analyze market prices from that viewpoint.

This is not to say that you are firmly and irrevocably bound by the standard of what you find the market for your kind of services to be: You are not yet making a final decision, and you are not bound totally by the market or by what anyone else does. There are always exceptions, and you will probably find a competitor or two who is leagues removed from what you have found to be the normal market. However, you can't completely disregard the normal market in making your analysis. At least consider this factor before reaching a decision.

Your Business Goals and Philosophy

Not the smallest factors in your analysis and decision are your own business goals and operating philosophy. Everyone sets personal standards of some sort. If the average billing rate in some field is $500 a day, you may be sure that this average ranges from limits of well under that to well over that fee, but you may also be sure that there are at least a few consultants charging several times that rate and getting it. I had little difficulty in charging clients $1,000 per day for helping them with their proposals. There are also marketing consultants who ask for and get $5,000 and more per day.

Worksheet 10.1. Setting rate standards.

1. Decide which of the following is your most typical—most frequently encountered or most likely to be encountered—assignment:

    ☐ Short-term, full-time and continuous effort
    ☐ Short-term, with intermittent efforts
    ☐ Medium-term, full-time and continuous effort
    ☐ Medium-term, with intermittent efforts
    ☐ Long-term, full-time and continuous effort
    ☐ Long-term, with intermittent effort

2. Which of the following is your principal marketplace?

    ☐ My local area
    ☐ The entire country
    ☐ The entire world

3. Which is your preferred business and marketing philosophy?

    ☐ A very busy schedule at modest rates for easier sales
    ☐ A light schedule at high rates, even if sales are harder to make
    ☐ An exceptionally high rate, regardless of sales effort needed
    ☐ Many bids for clearly defined projects at firm fixed prices
       ☐ Highly competitive in price
       ☐ Shooting for high prices
    ☐ Selective bids for clearly defined projects at firm fixed prices
       ☐ Highly competitive in price
       ☐ Shooting for high prices

4. What is your pricing policy?

    ☐ A daily rate
       ☐ For an indeterminate number of hours per day
       ☐ For 8 hours per day
       ☐ Rate is higher for more than 8 hours per day
       ☐ Same rate applies to weekends and holidays
       ☐ Rate is higher for weekend and holiday work
          ☐ Time and a half
          ☐ Double time
          ☐ _____

Worksheet 10.1.   Continued.

☐ An hourly rate
  ☐ Rate does not change for more than 8 hours per day
  ☐ Rate increased for more than 8 hours per day
  ☐ Rate higher for weekends and holidays
    ☐ Time and a half
    ☐ Double time
    ☐ _____

☐ Firm fixed price
  ☐ For-the-job flat price
    ☐ Based on maximum estimate
    ☐ Based on specifications
    ☐ Based on worst-case estimate
  ☐ Not-to-exceed ceiling
    ☐ Based on maximum estimate
    ☐ Based on specifications
    ☐ Based on worst-case estimate

There are trade-offs in setting your rates, of course. There is always the relationship between what you ask in the way of fees and the percentage of your leads you are able to close. Only once did a client say to me point-blank that my rate was too high for her to accept. However, undoubtedly my fee was a factor affecting sales. Or it affected how much the client asked me to do—how many days' work I was assigned.

One factor in fee setting is an emotional one, one of pride and self-esteem. There are individuals who think they demean themselves and belittle their own skills and contributions by accepting less than $5,000 per day for their services. (Or $10,000 and more, in many cases of "celebrity" consultants.) Perhaps these consultants all have elevated opinions of themselves, their images, and their worth. This characterization does fit some of them. Others set these high daily rates on a relatively unemotional basis. They are simply good promoters, marketers with great vision, and they believe that they can and do project a high-enough image of professionalism to justify the rates they ask.

The same philosophy applies to working on the basis of a clearly specified project at a firm fixed price. Some consultants prefer to pursue and bid for every project, relying in part on probability statistics, while others are highly selective in what they opt to pursue, carefully weighing the probability of success on various factors and making great efforts to do a superb marketing job. In either case, the consultant may bid very competitively—that is, work hard to be the low bidder—to maximize the probability of success in winning contracts. Others insist on taking on only those projects for which they can command a high price. To do this, they either bid most selectively—only for those contracts where they believe a high price quoted will not close out their chances of winning—or they submit many bids, under the theory that they can afford to lose most of them and capture the occasional one at a good enough price.

It is very much an individual matter. I found it possible to close enough sales at $1,000 per day to satisfy my wants, and I did not believe that I was cheapening my professional image by asking too low a fee.

ESTABLISHING A PRICING POLICY

The flat statement of so many dollars per hour or per day is not, of itself, completely definitive. The terms need further definition or qualification. If you work on a daily rate, how long is a "day?" Will you charge the client for all hours greater than eight in a working day? If so, at what rate will you charge those hours? What about working on weekends or holidays: Will that be at your stated daily rate? Similarly, if you charge by the hour, do you charge more for each hour worked in excess of eight per day or on holidays and weekends? All of these are factors that you will have to confront, sooner or later, and you can avoid the problem of appearing to be unprepared and uncertain when the questions arise if you think your way through these matters in advance and establish a policy.

The Rationale

No matter how experienced you are, unexpected situations arise. Planning means thinking out all the possible contingencies and preparing to cope with them by establishing a policy for each contingency. The fact of an established policy can help you avoid or at least retrieve some potentially embarrassing and awkward situations, perhaps even costly situations. Contingencies may arise where your most graceful exit is to plead established policy.

In my own consulting work, more than once I encountered the prospective client who wanted me to work on speculation: If the client won the contract, he would pay me a fee proportionate to the size of the contract, give me a profitable subcontract. I must confess to accepting such offers a few times, only to regret it each time. I finally established a firm policy and was henceforward able to state very quietly that it was my firm policy to accept assignments only on my established terms. That ended the matter without further discussion.

You may run into clients who wish to pay you on some basis other than the one you have established as your policy. Again, a quiet statement that you have a firm, established policy will end the discussion. It is the businesslike way to handle the problem. In fact, to the best of my knowledge, I never antagonized a prospective client or lost a sale by being pleasantly firm and insisting on following my own policies in doing business.

The Need for Flexibility

Some consultants will vary their rates and negotiate each assignment on the basis of trying for the highest rate the client is willing to pay and adjusting his or her asking price as necessary to win the contract. It is my own belief that it is better to stick with your established rates. Otherwise, the word may spread that you can be negotiated down, and you will then have a growing problem in winning work at your chosen rates. However, because your assignments can vary widely, it is possible that no single rate is suitable for all occasions. That is, you may have both short- and long-term assignments, requiring both hourly and daily rates, and you may have assignments that must be done on a fixed price basis.

Fixed-Price Qualifiers

The problem consultants often face in pricing is that the full scope of the client's requirement is difficult to establish. Quite often, the client is not able to furnish complete specifications nor even be very precise about even the partial specifications provided. The client may be stating simply a need to have something "fixed," "evaluated," or otherwise put in order, but be unable to tell you very much more than that in specifying the need. That uncertainty as to the full scope of the effort needed is alone a compelling reason for working on a daily or hourly rate. Understandably, you believe that you must have an open-ended contract because you cannot estimate or fairly establish how much time and effort you will require before the client's need is satisfied.

That arrangement may or may not be satisfactory to the client. Many clients—perhaps most clients—will want more control over the total cost, some guarantee that they are not granting you a blank check to fill out as you see fit. Clients will almost always want some guarantee of a satisfactory result and a concurrent guarantee that there is some maximum cost to which they are asked to agree. Providing such guarantees can be a dilemma, a rather common dilemma in consulting work, in fact. There are, however, at least three ways to resolve this dilemma of fixing a price without exposing yourself to an unacceptably large possibility of loss on the project:

1. As the consultant, you put a completely arbitrary not-to-exceed limit on the hours or days to be authorized. This limit represents your wild guess of the maximum effort—days or hours—necessary to get the job done. Obviously, the less certain you are of how many days or hours are going to be needed, the larger your estimate, to cover the contingency of your being completely wrong in your guesstimate. Of course, this may result in a rather firm objection by the client. You therefore have to have a fallback position (although it can as easily be your original position).

2. You have decided, as the consultant, what the need is, and have drawn up what you believe to be proper specifications for an effort to satisfy the need. You have made your best guess of what it will take to do the job, based your price on the specifications you propose, and have therefore agreed to a not-to-exceed contract or purchase order, at hourly or daily rates, based on your own stated specifications. These spell out in detail what you will do and, especially, what you will deliver as the end-product (for example, printed report and recommendations, computer tape, training program, training in kind, or other), and when you will deliver.

3. The client has, or you have persuaded the client, to provide the necessary hard and fast specifications, and on the basis of those you are ready to sign a firm, fixed-price contract, as fixed dollar amount. Even this amount is based on estimated hours of effort required plus whatever other expenses are involved, and the same clear statement of what and when you will deliver whatever it is the client has requested and you agree to. If other expenses are negligible—for example, telephone, copying, and typing—they can be absorbed by the overhead without penalty. If they are substantial, they should be included as "other direct costs."

Worksheet 10.1 provides space for you to establish a policy. That is, you can choose from among a number of options:

1. You may decide that you will work only on the basis of an hourly or daily rate and will not accept fixed-price work or not-to-exceed ceilings.
2. You may decide that you will accept fixed-price work, but only if you can agree with the client on an adequate set of specifications or worst-case estimate.
3. You may decide that you will accept work on any of the sets of conditions, according to the circumstances of the job.

Once you reach your decisions, you have a set of standards to help yourself analyze situations and come up quickly with the right response. (Of course, with experience, you may want to change your mind about much of this.)

Whatever your choices—but especially if you are willing to consider fixed-price projects—you need to gain an understanding of costs in business as you must project them in estimating a fixed-price job.

WHAT YOUR RATE SHOULD INCLUDE

One of the many mistakes the newcomer to business makes is to misunderstand overhead and what it means. In a rather broad definition, overhead is what it costs you to be in business and to stay in business. It includes those costs that you have regardless of how much or how little business you do. In practical terms, it means that you will not get to keep every dollar you collect from a client: Part of that dollar must go to keeping you in business. Obvious? Yes, but an amazingly large number of newcomers to business don't understand this fact.

There are also cases, such as in contracting with the federal government, when you are required to explain all the costs that make up your asking price, to reveal your overhead rate and the profit you ask for. Many consultants refuse to do business with any client who demands this information. However, there is a great deal of business to be had from government agencies at the federal, state, and local levels. If you wish to take advantage of the business opportunities offered by these agencies, you need to have at least a fundamental understanding of costs and cost accounting. And, of course, it is essential that you are aware of just what your income has to cover in order to stay in business.

There are two kinds of expenses generally. They are "direct" and "indirect." Indirect costs are those costs you cannot assign specifically to any specific job. They would usually include rent, heat, light, advertising, taxes, and miscellaneous costs. They are *overhead*, costs you have whether you are doing business or not, the cost of opening your doors every morning. Direct costs—*other* direct costs, in most cost breakdowns—would include such items as telephone, travel, printing, and any other costs that can be identified as incurred totally and only for a specific job. Good business judgment suggests that you ought to bill every client for direct expenses—for every expense that you can identify as being incurred for doing a job for a specific client. Other expenses, not identifiable as linked to specific projects, must be recovered by being assigned generally as overhead. That is, ignoring other direct costs for the moment, if you paid yourself $50,000 for 2,000 hours of labor and your other costs were $25,000, your total cost (including your own salary) was $75,000. Your overhead was $25,000 or 50 percent. Add 50 percent to your own salary, and your total cost is $75,000. Add a profit figure—a viable business must show a profit—of 15 percent, and you must bill your clients $50 (your salary) plus $25 (overhead costs) plus $11.25 (15% profit of $75), and your billing rate is $86.25.

Figure 10.1 offers a brief model of a cost presentation. It can get considerably more complex for the large organization and large project, but this is generally adequate for the smaller projects of the

Direct Labor

[Title] _____ hours   @ $_____ /hour $_____

[Title] _____ hours   @ $_____ /hour $_____ $_____

Overhead

$_____ direct labor   @ _____ % $_____ $_____

Other Direct Costs

_____ $_____

_____ $_____

Total Costs $_____

Fixed Fee or Profit: _____ % $_____ $_____

Total for the Job: $_____

Figure 10.1.   Cost presentation with total breakdown.

independent consultant. If you work alone, there may be only one line for the technical work, but you may need support help, clerical or other, and thus need additional lines to explain the payroll costs. Fee or profit may be percentage of the total cost or an arbitrary number. You are free to ask for either. Note that your own salary is cost, not profit. Each category of cost needs to be itemized, and then presented as a subtotal, with an overall total finally presented at the bottom.

11

The Financial Side of the Business

Most of us don't want to get involved in accounting or anything else that has to do with mathematics. However, it is not the numbers themselves that are the most significant aspect of accounting; it is what those numbers say about your business that makes them important. They sing to those who listen.

THE MUSIC OF THE NUMBERS

Many years ago a business associate, also self-employed and managing to achieve at least a modest success, said to me over lunch, "I find business a simple proposition. Keep doing whatever is profitable, and stop doing whatever is not profitable."

He said that with a large grin, which I shared, because we both knew that this was akin to the advice that the late Wall Street sage Bernard Baruch was alleged to have given someone who asked his formula for success in the stock market. Baruch was reported to have said, "It's really quite simple to make money in the stock market: Just buy low and sell high."

It is easy to say, "Keep doing what is profitable, and stop doing what is not profitable," and no one can challenge the basic wisdom of that formula. The trick, however, is knowing which is which, of course. Which operations are profitable or on their way to becoming profitable, and which are not? How can you make the distinction?

Even supercorporations—perhaps especially supercorporations—often insist on continuing operations that are not profitable and show no signs of ever being anything but drains on income and profits. It may happen because some individual executive's pride is involved: The original idea belonged to the executive, and that person is unable to believe that he or she was wrong. It may be that someone thinks, for whatever reason, that the operation will eventually become profitable, given enough time and effort. Perhaps—not an unlikely perhaps—no one in the company hierarchy is aware that the operation is a loser, and it can take a long time for that simple fact to surface in the right places to command the appropriate action.

One of the curses of the large corporation is that this kind of oversight can happen so easily and continue for so long. (IBM is one of the most recent and most prominent examples of this blindness, but it is not alone.) In a way, it is understandable that such oversight can occur in the supercorporation, for many reasons of no great interest here, but it ought never to happen in the small company, and certainly not in the one-person enterprise. Not if there is an appropriate accounting system in place, if the accounts are being maintained properly, and if the proprietor is using the accounting system as a major tool of management.

That latter condition is an important one. Accounting is a management tool, or ought to be. It may very well be the most important management tool available to you. Never underestimate its worth in that regard.

You don't have to be an accountant to understand accounting, and you don't have to be able to do all or any of the accounting work yourself, although accounting should not be complicated for a small venture, especially a one-person enterprise. Stated as simply and significantly as possible, accounting is a record and a report of how your business is doing. If it is kept accurately, it is the incorruptible report of how your business is doing. We humans can lie to each other and even to ourselves. We can rationalize and shade the truth. We can make apologies to ourselves and even pretend not to see or not to know unpleasant truths. The numbers in your accounting system, if it is a well-designed one, are immune to such influences. They tell you the truth. They tell you how much you have spent and where you have spent it. They tell you where and for what you have received income. They tell you what you are doing that is profitable and what is not profitable. They show you the trends: They show you the direction of various operations and various variable elements of your business. From this factual information you infer what changes you should make—what you should do more of and what you should stop doing—because they tell you what efforts and what expenditures produce income with profit, and which do not do so.

The feedback from this information also provides you with valuable marketing information, if you are "listening"—that is, taking the time and making the effort to analyze the music of the numbers:

- Which of your mailing pieces or print advertisements draw the most profitable reactions—produce clients and sales—and which do not?
- Which medium—periodical or mailing list—produces best for you?
- Which of your brochures is most effective?

If you structure your accounting and its feedback (reporting) system well, you can reduce risk to a minimum. You can ascertain quite specifically—almost scientifically—the answers to these and other questions:

- What offers to prospective clients do the prospects grasp most readily and which do they spurn?
- What do your markets want and what don't they want—that is, what attracts clients and assignments and what does not?
- Which markets or niches are most profitable for you and which are least profitable?

Why go to the expense of an elaborate and costly accounting system if you are not going to get these kinds of information—results—

from your system? (The IRS requirements can be satisfied by a quite primitive and inexpensive system.)

ACCOUNTING SYSTEMS

You have several choices for acquiring and installing a proper accounting system. You can buy a ready-made system that is suitable for a small business, and it can be a manual system or a computer system; most office supply emporiums can offer you an assortment of both. You can have a public accountant, preferably a certified one (CPA), set up your system for you. Or you can adopt some hybrid of these ideas, according to your own needs as you perceive them. My own case may shed some light.

I already had some experiences, mostly bad ones, in turning over my accounting needs to a public accountant. I had been disappointed and dissatisfied, and had finally resorted to running my own manual system, using the forms and records it provided and those I had bought in a local office supply store. But when I later incorporated, to solve a problem with the IRS, I felt a need for professional help because accounting for a corporation is more complex than accounting for a simple sole proprietorship, such as I had been running. I was, however, somewhat wary when I decided to talk to an accountant recommended to me by a business acquaintance whose judgment I respected.

Marty, my accountant-to-be, was a principal in a small accounting firm that had enough names in its title to be a large accounting firm, perhaps even a major law firm. Marty was sincere and eager to help, especially since he handled accounting for those who had sent me to him. He described a marvelous system he proposed to install for me. I demurred, insisting that I neither needed nor wanted a cradle-to-the-grave system. In fact, I was somewhat intimidated by the prospect of having such a magnificent system. It would have been entirely suitable to a small corporation of a few dozen or perhaps a few hundred employees, but quite formidable for a one-man venture. I insisted that it was gross overkill and despite my awe, I was not at all willing to have Marty make my decisions for me. I insisted that I would keep my own books, continuing with my Dome® manual system, and I would deliver my books to him to do my taxes for me. We argued for a while, but Marty finally surrendered to my wishes. That was considerably more than a dozen years ago, and our relationship has continued on that basis since, so the idea must have been viable enough. You do not have to have an elaborate system (I am sure I could have finally persuaded Marty to install a simpler system for me, had I wished it), and you do not have to turn it all over to an accountant if you do not wish to. But let me elaborate on why I did not want to have Marty or any other accountant keep my books.

My greatest discontent with my earlier experiences with a public accountant was the length of time it took for feedback to reach me. At best, it was mid- to late May before I knew how I had done in March, for example. If I had some losing operation or was wasting money on some expenditure, I wanted to know before two months had elapsed. I didn't believe that I could afford to go on for two or more months doing the wrong things. The only way I could avoid that, as far as I could see, was to keep my own log and ledger. (How much closer to your business can you get?)

If you have trouble understanding your accounts and determining what they mean to you in simple language, it may be that you are using a system that is far more complex and sophisticated than you need—one that is not suitable for you. You almost surely need only a simple, straightforward system, and a simple system should be simple to understand.

Of course, you don't have to run your system manually. Today, there are many small accounting programs you can run on a PC, whether you do your own taxes or not. The taxes may be somewhat complicated, especially if you incorporate, but the books are not complicated unless you make them so. There is a daily log or diary in which you enter every transaction—each dollar out and each dollar in—every day, as it happens. Once a week or once a month, however you have set up your system, you add up the information in the daily log and transfer the totals, by category, to your ledgers, where you total and balance the figures.

Surely, you don't have to be a Phi Beta Kappa to master that idea.

THE NEED FOR START-UP CAPITAL

As stated earlier, most people setting themselves up as independent consultants do not experience any large or extraordinary front-end or investment costs. That does not mean that you may not be an exception, or that even if you are not an exception, that you will have no front-end costs. You will, of course, have some kind of initial investment cost, even if some of that cost was expended earlier—that is, if you already own office furniture and equipment as personal property. Making them business property—making business assets out of personal assets—is part of your front-end investment. Let's look first at the major items that make up your capital needs for a typical independent consultancy. Consider Worksheets 11.1 and 11.2 as general models, although they will have to be adapted to whatever the needs are of your own consulting specialty.

A Needs List

Worksheet 11.1 lists the typical minimal needs for setting up and equipping an office, such as it is presumed you will need. What are listed are the simple, garden variety items most offices require. Space is provided to add other items, perhaps special items, that you will need, such as a drawing board, light table, drafting tools, or other items that are special requirements for your own consulting discipline.

Study this worksheet carefully. You want to list here everything you will need to "open your doors" as an independent consultant, but you will not want to have anything unnecessary (unless you are amply provided with capital and wish to be careless with it).

Capital Items Inventory

These lists will help you fill out Worksheet 11.2, which will help you to begin to arrive at some estimates of the start-up capital you will require, beginning with the needs of your office. Your office will

Worksheet 11.1.   Initial needs list.

1. Office furniture and fixtures:

   ☐ Desk   ☐ Chair   ☐ Filing cabinet   ☐ Bookcase
   ☐ _____
   ☐ _____

2. Office equipment:

   ☐ Computer
   ☐ Printer
   ☐ Typewriter
   ☐ Fax
   ☐ Calculator
   ☐ Adding machine with paper tape
   ☐ Postage meter
   ☐ Telephone
   ☐ Copier
   ☐ Answering machine
   ☐ _____
   ☐ _____

3. Computer supplies:

   ☐ Software
      ☐ Word processor   ☐ Database manager
      ☐ Spreadsheet   ☐ Accounting program
      ☐ _____
      ☐ _____
   ☐ Floppy disks   ☐ CD ROM disks   ☐ Computer tool kit
   ☐ _____
   ☐ _____

4. General office supplies:

   ☐ Stationery   ☐ Fax paper   ☐ Printer paper
   ☐ Books and manuals
      ☐ Dictionary   ☐ Reference books   ☐ Technical manuals
   ☐ _____
   ☐ _____

5. Marketing supplies:

   ☐ Business cards   ☐ Stationery   ☐ Brochures
   ☐ _____
   ☐ _____

Worksheet 11.2.   Assessment of initial capital required.

1. The physical facility, an office:

Furniture
☐ Already have
    ☐ Fair value $ _____
    ☐ Must buy
    ☐ Estimated cost $ _____ $ _____

Fixtures
☐ Already have
    ☐ Fair value $ _____
☐ Must buy
    ☐ Estimated cost $ _____ $ _____

Equipment
☐ Already have
    ☐ Fair value $ _____
☐ Must buy
    ☐ Estimated cost $ _____ $ _____

Estimated total capitalization $ _____

Estimated initial cash required for
    purchases of capital items $ _____

2. Supplies (initial stock):

Computer
☐ Estimated costs $ _____

Office
☐ Estimated cost $ _____

Marketing
☐ Estimated costs $ _____

    Subtotal $ _____

Estimated total cash required
    for start-up $ _____

probably represent your major capital-items list, as it does for most independent consultants beginning a home-based practice.

If you have to buy these items, you will have to project the costs. In many cases, probably most, the independent consultant starts out with either many of these items already existent as personal property or with personal property that can be used. For example, a desk need not be that piece of furniture normally known as a desk in the business world; it can be a table that is pressed into use as a desk. You may have a personal computer that is not the ideal one for business use, but it can serve you and your business for a while. The same principle applies for calculators, bookshelves, filing cabinets, and other normal appurtenances of the business office. Certainly it is wise to minimize your needs for hard cash in the beginning. Use what you have, if it can serve the purpose, and wait until the business can itself begin to pay for the more refined and effective models of your various requirements. However, do place a reasonable value on whatever contributions you make to the business in kind, rather than in cash. These are part of your initial investment, and should become assets of the business. (You must begin to think in terms of "the business" as an entity in itself.)

You want to make two totals. One will be the total estimated cost of whatever you have determined you must buy immediately to get started. Do that first for the capital items, furniture, fixtures, and equipment. That figure represents part of the cash and/or credit you will need for your start-up. At the same time, add to that figure the estimated fair value of whatever personal property you are using for your start-up. If a fair market value for your personal computer is $2,000, for example, use that figure. That is part of what you are using to capitalize your business. It is as much a part of your investment as is the cash you put into your business start-up. That, plus the cost of those items you must buy (even if you must buy them on credit), represents your capital items list and capital asset. You will have to list these in your accounts and depreciate them as the law and accepted accounting practice dictates. Your accountant will guide you or do this for you.

It may be that you will not have to buy any capital items initially. You may be able to get started with what you already own. Even so, it makes good sense to "sell" those items to your business—make them part of your original investment. Remember, you and your business are separate entities, philosophically, even if you have not incorporated your business. The business must employ you and pay you a draw or salary as part of the cost of doing business. (Be sure you understand that your salary is part of the cost of doing business, and is not part of profit.) Even if you are a sole proprietor, which is the least complicated way to set up your business organization, it is best to think of the business as a separate entity that must stand on its own feet, pay you a salary, satisfy all its costs, and realize some profit. (Profit is not a dirty word. It's what a business needs to grow, to cover contingencies, and to survive disasters that come along inevitably.)

WORKING CAPITAL

One financial item you must not overlook in your planning is that of working capital. You may not need substantial working capital, of course, if you have some independent source of income (for example, a working spouse who earns enough to support your family) or are starting your practice with one or more clients and contracts that will produce a cash flow almost immediately. If you are not that fortunate, you must anticipate a period of time before you win your first clients and begin to enjoy a cash flow. That can, in fact, be a rather long time.

Your Salary

Conventional thinking is that you should be prepared to support yourself independently of cash flow from your new business for at least one year, and that is considered by many to be not long enough. The assumption upon which that advice is based is that your business will not even reach breakeven in the first year, and quite possibly not for several years. That reasoning, however, is derived from the typical histories of manufacturing and product-oriented businesses, and is not a reliable model for consulting and other service businesses. If you have planned well and chosen your start-up time wisely, you should be able to do much better than that and perhaps even hit the ground running, as a great many independent consultants do. That estimate is probably excessively conservative for an independent consultancy, especially one that is home-based. If you are home-based, you get a double advantage that greatly eases what would otherwise be a heavy burden: You avoid having rent and other extra expenses of an office away from your home, and if you can properly dedicate the space at home for an office, you can write its cost off as a tax-deductible expense. (You can also enjoy tax benefits by prorating other costs at home for business purposes.)

Despite all these measures, to maximize your prospects for a successful venture, you should allow for some period of time before your venture is on solid footing. However, being able to draw a salary during the early months is not the only consideration for working capital. There are other needs for capital you must anticipate.

Marketing Expenses

Marketing is not only one of the most important activities of any business, especially at the onset, it is also one of the most expensive activities of many businesses. Both of these observations are almost certainly true of an independent consulting practice. It would probably be a rare one of which these things could not be said.

A great many businesses rely on advertising of various sorts, print and broadcast most commonly, but also direct mail, to pursue their marketing goals. Unfortunately, this approach to marketing—pursuing prospective clients, that is—does not normally work well for independent consultants. The probability is, therefore, that you will not incur a large advertising cost even initially, unless you choose to have a prominent notice in the yellow pages of your local telephone directory or you wish to use advertising to make announcements, such as offering a seminar and inviting readers to write or call for a free newsletter or other handout created to help build a mailing list. Other than that—that is, with regard to general advertising of consulting services—there seems to be little confirmation that such notices pay off for the average independent consultant because while most of us pursue business firms as our clients, few business firms turn to print advertising of any sort to find experts when they find themselves in need of such counsel, guidance, and service as consultants normally provide. How, then, do executives seek out consultants?

The fact is that probably few executives ever consciously start out to find a consultant. Far more often it is the consultant who finds the client. Consultants find clients through networking, public speaking, writing, and whatever other methods consultants can use to make their presence and the services they offer known to those who are most likely to need those services. The latter may not even be aware of that need until they learn of the service available. For example, it may not occur to an executive whose computer is not doing a great job for him that a computer consultant can greatly improve the machine's performance.

In short, the most effective marketing tools you can use are probably those that make prospects aware of your existence and what you do through means other than paid advertising. Those tools include writing for the trade and professional journals, public speaking at events in your industry, and service in relevant associations, to name three major activities that raise your level of visibility.

The problem with most of these activities is that they are not under your control to any degree but a very small one. They are highly dependent on the cooperation of others, those who are the association executives and publishers. They are, therefore, far more reactive than proactive. That does not preclude you from using proactive methods. You can control your writing and speaking activities by sponsoring your own seminars and publishing your own newsletter and monographs, for example, as just two examples of how you can seize the initiative and take control.

Seminar Planning and Costing

Worksheet 11.3 will help you plan speaking and writing activities that you can control. Staging the seminars suggested does not preclude you from speaking on any and every other occasion you can, and it does furnish you with a certain method that you can control.

Worksheet 11.3.   Planning seminars.

1. Seminar production and presentation:
   - ☐ Full day
   - ☐ Half-day
   - ☐ Less than half-day

2. Sites and occasions:
   - ☐ Normal business days
   - ☐ Weekends
   - ☐ Conventions, other special occasions
   - ☐ _____

3. Number of days and frequency:
   - ☐ 1 day
   - ☐ _____ days
   - ☐ Monthly
   - ☐ Quarterly

4. Estimated cost:
   - ☐ Room rental $ _____
   - ☐ Equipment rental   _____
   - ☐ Refreshments   _____
   - ☐ Presentation materials   _____
     - ☐ Posters   _____
     - ☐ Slides   _____
     - ☐ Transparencies   _____
     - ☐ Handouts   _____
   - ☐ Publicity for the seminars   _____
     - ☐ Advertising   _____
     - ☐ Brochures   _____
     - ☐ Press releases   _____
   - Total $ _____

Note that the worksheet makes provision for seminars from a short period, such as one or two hours, to a half-day or full day. The choice is entirely yours, but there are some pertinent observations that should be made.

You probably should not attempt to collect a fee for your seminars when you are new and still feeling your way. In any case, we are talking about seminars as a marketing tool, so we will assume here that these are presentations made at your expense to make the world of prospects aware of your presence and what you have to offer. They are seminars, but they are also sales presentations: That is their ultimate purpose.

It is probably best to keep your initial presentations relatively short, preferably one hour and not more than two. (A half-day seminar is normally three hours.) It may be difficult, even in a free seminar, to attract and hold an audience for much more than an hour. But there is another consideration: With a one-hour seminar, you can deliver it at least five or six times a day to five or six audiences. That frequency alone is a powerful argument for the brief seminar, if it is to be used as a marketing tool.

The use of a seminar as a marketing tool is an important consideration. It is relatively easy to attract an audience for a short presentation for which you make no charge, but by that same token, a great many people who attend will be idle curiosity seekers, resting their weary feet or killing time and not serious prospects for what you offer. The more people you address each day, the greater the probability that you will get substantial results—good sales leads and clients. In general, marketing of all kinds depends more on probability statistics—reaching maximum numbers of prospects—than on any other single factor.

You may want to do this sort of thing on only one day or on several days. And you may want to repeat your seminars every month or every quarter until you have reached a point where you have enough sales and clients to permit you to market with considerably less frenzy. The worksheet provides the flexibility to plan either way, and you can, of course, change your plans at any time.

Finally, you will want to decide what, if any, refreshments you will offer attendees and what you will need in the way of presentation materials and handouts. Project your estimates of the costs of these things.

Planning and Costing Publications

This is a good time to plan any publications you wish to produce to support your marketing efforts. Worksheet 11.4 describes some of the choices available, primarily along the two parameters of number of pages and frequency of publication.

The assumption is that your newsletter will be of the conventional size, 8½ by 11 inches per page, although some newsletter publishers prefer the tabloid size. In arriving at estimates of cost, check

Worksheet 11.4. Planning for publication costs.

1. Newsletters:
   - ☐ Size
     - ☐ 8.5 × 11 inches
     - ☐ Tabloid
   - ☐ Number of pages
     - ☐ 2
     - ☐ 4
     - ☐ 8
     - ☐ _____
   - ☐ Frequency of publication
     - ☐ Monthly $ _____
     - ☐ Bimonthly   _____
     - ☐ Quarterly   _____
     - ☐ _____   _____

2. Brochures
   - ☐ Format
     - ☐ 3 × 9 inches
     - ☐ 5.5 × 8.5 inches
     - ☐ 9 × 12 inches
   - ☐ Number of pages
     - ☐ 4 $ _____
     - ☐ 8   _____
     - ☐ 12   _____
     - ☐ _____   _____

with your local printer on printing and collating costs. Your printer can suggest to you the many choices of paper, inks, and other variables that affect the cost.

It is not necessary to publish your newsletter every month, especially if you are giving it away as a marketing device. It will be far less costly and almost as effective if you make it a bimonthly or even quarterly publication and distribute it throughout the period.

To keep costs down, do not plan on using photographs or other material of continuous tone. Such originals must be screened to make printing plates, adding considerably to cost. On the other hand, there is no penalty attached to using line drawings and charts. Use these as freely as you wish.

Brochures offer the same wide range of choices and costs as do newsletter possibilities. These are far more than can be presented in a simple worksheet. Your printer will show you many samples and quote you prices to help you make your own ballpark estimates.

There are other items you may wish to consider as income producers. For example, some consultants I have met have created sets of audio tapes, usually with an accompanying manual, and sell these to clients at excellent prices. Such tapes are, in fact, a prime source of income for many specialists, and they sell these sets by mail, through their newsletters, and at their seminars.

INCOME PROJECTIONS

Two Purposes

Now that you have developed cost projections for start-up in minimum configuration, and with the addition of certain marketing refinements, projections of income are in order, based on estimates of yearly operations for three years. These projections will serve two useful purposes:

1. They will tell you how much start-up capital you need for a basic or minimal starting configuration—that is, minimal

initial investment—and for maximal or intermediate start-up configurations—that is, with a program that includes one or more major marketing initiatives.

2. They will tell you at what points in the development of your venture you will be able to afford to add any additional activities that you cannot afford at start-up.

These will be estimates, of course, projected for planning purposes. They may or may not be close to actuality, depending largely on whether you are developing a business plan for a practice already in existence, one for which you already have some historical data, or one still in contemplation. In either case, as in all estimating, be prepared to review your estimates periodically and adjust them to match reality.

A Third Purpose

Although there are the stated two major purposes for making these estimates, in actuality there is a third purpose that may be of major importance in some cases: What you opt to install in your configuration and when you choose to do so is up to you. You may decide in advance to start with the smallest possible initial investment and build slowly, adding additional features and activities little by little, or you may decide in advance that you want to start with a full program of advertising, convention exhibits, seminars, publications, and other activities. In either case, making income projections will help you judge how much cash you will need for your startup. It will tell you how much cash you need to raise, if you do not have enough cash on hand for whatever starting configuration you decide you want.

Despite the premise that most independent consultants require relatively little cash for investment in their enterprises, there are exceptions, and it is for these exceptions that this coverage has been saved until now. If you are going to go outside your personal assets to start a consulting practice, you need to prepare for this in advance.

Outside Financing

There are two general kinds of financing to consider, *debt financing* and *equity financing*. Put as simply as possible, debt financing is borrowing money with an obligation to pay it back according to an agreement you enter into—acquiring one or more debts, that is. Equity financing is financing achieved by having others invest in your business, which gives them an equity interest in your business. But using outside financing is not necessarily an either-or situation: Many entrepreneurs use both kinds of financing.

Raising capital, particularly an initial investment in a service-based enterprise, is not easy. Conventional sources of capital, banks especially, tend to favor quite strongly the venture that can point to an inventory of goods and seem not to understand the assets of a service business. But venture capitalists and other investors are also highly practical people, and are cautious about the risks they accept.

Admittedly, it is not too likely that you will want to seek equity financing. The very spirit that leads individuals to launch their ventures as independent consultants is one that tends to want complete control. On the other hand, debt financing, borrowing from banks, is not easy, as noted already, for any small business, especially a start-up.

Doing the Figuring

You will need certain financial data if you are going to seek outside financing, but it is data you should have prepared in any case. One of the things you should do is make income projections. Worksheet 11.5 will help you make these projections. Estimates you made earlier, in other worksheets, will be of help to you now in making projections of income.

Refer to Worksheet 10.1, in which you developed a structure and standard for setting your rates, but were not asked to assign dollar figures at that point. However, to project income, you must now

Worksheet 11.5.   Gross income projections, sheet 1.

First Year/Quarter

1. Rates for service:

   ☐ Daily rate, normal business days $ _____

   ☐ Daily rate, weekends and holidays $ _____

   ☐ Hourly rate, normal business hours $ _____

   ☐ Hourly rate, weekends and holidays $ _____

2. Estimated billable days/hours per week:

   _____ days/hrs @ $ _____ /day/hr $ _____

   _____ days/hrs @ $ _____ /day/hr $ _____

   Subtotal $ _____

3. Income from other activities:

   ☐ Seminars

   _____ attendees   @ $_____ $ _____

   ☐ Newsletter

   _____ subscriptions   @ $_____ $ _____

   ☐ Manuals/reports

   _____ manuals/reports @ $_____ $ _____

   Other _____   @ $ _____ $ _____

   Subtotal $ _____

   Grand total $ _____

Worksheet 11.5.   Gross income projections, sheet 2.

Second Year/Quarter

1. Rates for service:

    ☐ Daily rate, normal business days $ _____
    ☐ Daily rate, weekends and holidays $ _____
    ☐ Hourly rate, normal business hours $ _____
    ☐ Hourly rate, weekends and holidays $ _____

2. Estimated billable days/hours per week:

    _____ days/hrs @ $ _____ /day/hr $ _____
    _____ days/hrs @ $ _____ /day/hr $ _____

                                    Subtotal $ _____

3. Income from other activities:

    ☐ Seminars
       _____ attendees   @ $_____ $ _____

    ☐ Newsletter
       _____ subscriptions   @ $_____ $ _____

    ☐ Manuals/reports
       _____ manuals/reports @ $_____ $ _____
    Other _____   @ $ _____ $ _____

                                    Subtotal $ _____

                                    Grand total $ _____

Worksheet 11.5.　Gross income projections, sheet 3.

Third Year/Quarter

1.　Rates for service:

　　☐ Daily rate, normal business days　　　$ _____
　　☐ Daily rate, weekends and holidays　　$ _____
　　☐ Hourly rate, normal business hours　　$ _____
　　☐ Hourly rate, weekends and holidays　　$ _____

2.　Estimated billable days/hours per week:

　　_____ days/hrs @ $ _____ /day/hr　　$ _____
　　_____ days/hrs @ $ _____ /day/hr　　$ _____

　　　　　　　　　　　　　　　　　Subtotal　　$ _____

3.　Income from other activities:

　　☐ Seminars
　　　　_____ attendees　　　@ $_____　　$ _____

　　☐ Newsletter
　　　　_____ subscriptions　@ $_____　　$ _____

　　☐ Manuals/reports
　　　　_____ manuals/reports @ $_____　　$ _____

　　Other _____　@ $ _____　　$ _____

　　　　　　　　　　　　　　　　　Subtotal　　$ _____

　　　　　　　　　　　　　　　　　Grand total　$ _____

Worksheet 11.5.   Gross income projections, sheet 4.

Fourth Year/Quarter

1. Rates for service:

    ☐ Daily rate, normal business days $ _____
    ☐ Daily rate, weekends and holidays $ _____
    ☐ Hourly rate, normal business hours $ _____
    ☐ Hourly rate, weekends and holidays $ _____

2. Estimated billable days/hours per week:

    _____ days/hrs @ $ _____ /day/hr $ _____
    _____ days/hrs @ $ _____ /day/hr $ _____

                                          Subtotal $ _____

3. Income from other activities:

    ☐ Seminars
        _____ attendees   @ $_____ $ _____

    ☐ Newsletter
        _____ subscriptions   @ $_____ $ _____

    ☐ Manuals/reports
        _____ manuals/reports @ $_____ $ _____
    Other _____   @ $ _____ $ _____

                                          Subtotal $ _____

                                          Grand total $ _____

Worksheet 11.5.   Gross income projections, sheet 5.

Second Year

1. Rates for service:

   ☐ Daily rate, normal business days $ _____

   ☐ Daily rate, weekends and holidays $ _____

   ☐ Hourly rate, normal business hours $ _____

   ☐ Hourly rate, weekends and holidays $ _____

2. Estimated billable days/hours per week:

   _____ days/hrs @ $ _____ /day/hr $ _____

   _____ days/hrs @ $ _____ /day/hr $ _____

                                            Subtotal $ _____

3. Income from other activities:

   ☐ Seminars

      _____ attendees   @ $_____ $ _____

   ☐ Newsletter

      _____ subscriptions   @ $_____ $ _____

   ☐ Manuals/reports

      _____ manuals/reports @ $_____ $ _____

   Other _____   @ $ _____ $ _____

                                            Subtotal $ _____

                                            Grand total $ _____

Worksheet 11.5.   Gross income projections, sheet 6.

Third Year

1. Rates for service:

    ☐ Daily rate, normal business days $ _____
    ☐ Daily rate, weekends and holidays $ _____
    ☐ Hourly rate, normal business hours $ _____
    ☐ Hourly rate, weekends and holidays $ _____

2. Estimated billable days/hours per week:

    _____ days/hrs @ $ _____ /day/hr $ _____
    _____ days/hrs @ $ _____ /day/hr $ _____

                                                Subtotal $ _____

3. Income from other activities:

    ☐ Seminars
        _____ attendees   @ $_____ $ _____

    ☐ Newsletter
        _____ subscriptions   @ $_____ $ _____

    ☐ Manuals/reports
        _____ manuals/reports @ $_____ $ _____
    Other _____   @ $ _____ $ _____

                                                Subtotal $ _____

                                                Grand total $ _____

---

decide on the actual numbers—the dollar values at which you will set your rates. You must decide whether you will charge daily or hourly rates, although you may find it expedient to have both daily and hourly fees. You will also decide whether you will charge premiums for overtime and work outside of normal business days and hours, or charge high enough rates to permit you the luxury of a single rate for each. (Yes, it is a luxury in that it greatly simplifies your bookkeeping. But it is also a marketing advantage in that you can point to it as a benefit to your clients.)

If you decide to charge premium rates for services rendered outside of normal business days and hours, you may wish to follow popularly accepted practices. They are one and one-half times the normal rate for overtime on business days and for Saturday work, and double the normal rate for work on Sundays and holidays. If you normally charge a daily fee and are asked to work a few hours of overtime, you will have to decide how to bill that time, by the hour or as a fraction of a day. For example, if your daily fee is $600 and you work two hours overtime on a given day, you can break your daily fee down into an hourly rate—$600/8 = $75/hour; ergo, two hours overtime equals $750 for the day. You may therefore bill that as 1¼ days. "Ten hours" amounts to the same thing, of course, but you may prefer to keep all your billing in terms of days as the billing unit.

Worksheet 11.5 does not provide entries for income from fixed-price jobs and other larger projects. However, the principle is the same. If you make up a detailed costs estimate (Figure 10.1), such as government agencies and others are likely to require for large projects, you still should bill your time at the standard rates you've established.

Basis for Estimates

If you have been in practice for a time, you have your own business history to use as a basis for estimating your billable hours for the next year, on average. Worksheet 11.5 is based on the premise that you will project year-around averages, and the totals for items 2 and 3 are for the year. However, in some cases, performing consulting services is a seasonal matter, with busy seasons and slow seasons. In proposal writing, serving clients who focus primarily on government contracts, for example, there is normally a definite busy season during the third quarter of the government fiscal year, when many agencies accelerate their spending before the fiscal year ends and they must return any portions of their budgets left unspent. A marketing consultant might find the late spring and early summer slow seasons. If large seasonal fluctuations are the norm in your own practice, and you expect substantial differences due to that factor, you may find it beneficial to make these projections in terms of quarters, rather than of the year.

For that reason, there are six sheets to Worksheet 11.5. The first four sheets are provided for four quarters, if you wish to estimate on that basis, with two more so that you can add projections for the second and third years. Note, too, that provision is made to change your rate structures and standards, if experience suggests a need to do so.

Some financial managers suggest that for a small, new venture, it is a good idea to make income projections on a monthly basis for the first year. If you wish to do that, simply make additional copies of the worksheet and modify it to indicate that it is a monthly projection.

CASH NEEDS CALCULATION

Now you are ready to determine what your real needs will be for cash to start your practice. Worksheet 11.6 is provided to help you collect your figures from previous estimates. Fill in your first-year income projection from Worksheet 11.5 (sheet 1). Go back to worksheets 11.2, 11.3, and 11.4 and insert into the proper spaces on Worksheet 11.6 the amount of money you will need for a minimal start-up and for the added activities. This exercise is not to add up your total investment but to determine how much cash you will need for that investment. Here, you can begin to see the balance between costs projections and income projections. You can also begin to see why you may have to phase in all the "extras" of seminars, publications, and other items gradually because they cost front money to produce, unlike your service, which costs your time but no extra out-of-pocket cost.

Worksheet 11.6.   Cash needs calculation.

1. Income projection, first year:
   - ☐ Services $ _____
   - ☐ Seminars $ _____
   - ☐ Publications $ _____
   - ☐ Other $ _____

   Total $ _____

2. Costs, first year:
   - ☐ Minimal start-up $ _____
   - ☐ Seminars $ _____
   - ☐ Publications $ _____
   - ☐ Other $ _____

   Total $ _____

   Investment Required $ _____

SUMMARIZING YOUR FINANCIAL DATA
Balance Sheet

A balance sheet summarizes the state of your business at any given time—at whatever time you cast the balance sheet (see Figure 11.1). In business plans, it tends to be placed usually at or near the back of the plan. The balance sheet enables anyone to determine at a glance the state of your enterprise and its condition—assets and liabilities, liquidity, debt-equity ratio, and net worth. (Investors and lenders are likely to want to see balance sheets on a quarterly basis, at least for the first couple of years.)

Current assets include cash on hand, accounts receivable, inventories, prepaid expenses, securities, and anything else that can or will be converted to cash in the course of conducting your business. Fixed assets are furniture, fixtures, equipment, software, and other items that have a value. (Remember that earlier you decided what personal

Balance Sheet

Company Name _____

Date _____

Assets

Current		$ _____
Fixed	$_____	
Less depreciation	$_____	
Net fixed assets		$ _____
Other Assets		$ _____
Total Assets		$ _____

Liabilities

Current	$ _____
Long-Term	$ _____
Total Liabilities	$ _____
Net Worth (assets minus liabilities = owner's equity)	$ _____
Total Liabilities and Net Worth	$ _____

Figure 11.1.   Format for balance sheet.

possessions of yours could be used for business purposes, and thus transferred to your business at whatever their fair value was. The sum of those values is part of your initial investment, and should be reflected in your financial statement.) Most such assets have a value that declines with age, and is thus depreciated in its "book value" each year. It is thus lessened as an asset each year until its book value reaches zero, for tax purposes. There are also other assets you may have—intangibles such as licenses, patents, copyrights, and options.

Current liabilities include accounts payable, taxes owed, currently due installments of long-term debt, and other items due during the current business year. Long-term liabilities are mortgages and long-term loans, including installment purchases of equipment.

The total of assets minus liabilities equals your equity, also referred to as net worth. That is an important number to you, but the ratio of assets to liabilities is a most important figure to anyone contemplating a loan or investment.

Liquidity is an element of great interest to anyone examining the state of your business. It is a measure of the ability of your business to meet its immediate obligations out of cash on hand or assets readily convertible to cash. Should you find yourself in need of outside financing, you will need an up-to-date balance sheet.

In practice, a balance sheet tends to be more detailed than the simple format of Figure 11.1 indicates. It would identify the items listed in much more detail, as in Figure 11.2, although as an indepen-

---

Balance Sheet

Company Name _____

Date _____

Assets		**Liabilities**	
Current assets	$ _____	Current liabilities	$ _____
Cash	$ _____	Accounts payable	$ _____
Accounts receivable	$ _____	Current payments	
Inventory	$ _____	on long-term debt	$ _____
Supplies	$ _____		
Prepaid expenses	$ _____	Total current liabilities	$ _____
		Long-term liabilities	$ _____
Total current assets	$ _____	Note payable	$ _____
Fixed assets	$ _____	Bank loan payable	$ _____
Furniture and fixtures	$ _____		
Equipment	$ _____	Total long-term	
Software	$ _____	liabilities	$ _____
Reference library	$ _____	Net worth	
		Owner's equity	$ _____
Total fixed assets	$ _____		
		Total liabilities and	
Total assets	$ _____	net worth	$ _____

Figure 11.2. Detailed balance sheet.

dent consultant you may or may not have an inventory of merchandise, and "supplies" might well be a negligible item. If you have no investors and have not borrowed money, you will have no notes or payments to make. You will therefore have as assets your furniture and fixtures, equipment, software, cash on hand, and receivables, and your liabilities will be current debt, primarily accounts payable. If you have bought capital items on an installment plan, however, you will have that as a long-term debt, with the payment due at the time representing a liability. It is a practice to footnote a balance sheet to supply the necessary details.

The bottom line of each category—total assets and total liabilities and net worth—must be the same figure, balancing each other. That is inevitable because net worth, your equity, is the difference between total assets and total liability.

Profit and Loss Statement

An income statement, more often referred to as a "profit and loss statement," is another document lenders and investors want to see. Figure 11.3 is an example of such a statement in a generally accepted format. You may not have all the items. "General and administrative costs," commonly referred to as G&A in the business world, is an item of indirect costs analogous to, but separate from and in addition to, overhead costs. However, it is not included as an item in all businesses and accounting systems and is much more appropriate and relevant to multibranch corporations with central headquarters facilities than it is to the independent consultancy. So it's not likely that you'll have this item in your accounting system. Rather, your indirect expenses will probably all be covered as overhead. (Some accounting systems include all indirect costs in an overhead expense pool, while others break overhead down into two pools, one of them fringe benefits for employees—paid time off, bonuses, insurance, and other—and the other including all other indirect costs. For an independent consultancy, it probably makes good sense to keep the system simple and count all indirect costs as overhead.)

Profit and Loss Statement

Company Name _____

Date _____

Sales		$_____
Cost of Sales		
Material	$_____	
Labor	$_____	
Overhead	$_____	
Total Cost of Sales		$_____
Gross Margin		
Sales less cost of sales		$_____
Operating Expenses		
Marketing and selling costs	$_____	
Research & development	$_____	
General and administrative costs	$_____	
Other expenses	$_____	
Total Operating Expenses	$_____	
Income (Loss)		$_____
Taxes		$_____
Net Income (Loss)		$_____

Figure 11.3. Profit and loss statement.

WHERE TO GO FROM HERE

This has been a relatively cursory examination of the financial aspects of an independent consultant's business plan. That is not because the independent consultant's business venture is not a serious one deserving of serious attention. It does, obviously, deserve that attention. There is, however, a distinct difference between the modest venture requiring a few thousand dollars, at most, for its launch and the venture requiring several hundred thousand dollars for even a minimal start-up. For me to have gone into the myriad details of financial statements—with cash flow projections, break-even analyses, and other such presentations necessary for the financing of major undertakings—would have taken us far beyond actual needs. If yours is that truly rare exception that requires big bucks to launch, you will need a plan far more ambitious in detail than you have read about here. Guidance for those more ambitious quests is furnished in the appendix, where there are listed a number of other resources that should be of use to you, whatever your immediate needs.

12

A Sample Business Plan

"For-instances" are often the most effective tools for learning.

The business plan for a small venture, such as an independent consultancy, is not a long and impressive document. There is normally no need for it to be other than a modest document. The work lies in gathering the information—the estimates, the analyses, and the calculations that we have been through in all the preceding pages. The written plan then summarizes all of this data relatively succinctly. In fact, it is very much in your interest that it be as succinct as possible, if it is to serve you well for periodic review to remind you of what you planned and how you intended to carry out your plans and meet your goals.

The following sample is based on my own tiny corporation, with a bit of imaginative expansion to exemplify some of the typical diversification of a consulting practice. Since a great many consultants also write and speak publicly—the three functions seem to be natural complements for each other—it is not always easy for even the practitioner to be sure which is the major function and which the ancillary ones.

Financial projections follow the text. It is, of course, highly speculative to cast projections five years in advance, especially for a new business without a history. However, the figures are to be reexamined regularly and new estimates made as experience and history accumulate.

A BUSINESS PLAN FOR
HRH COMMUNICATIONS INC.

EXECUTIVE SUMMARY

HRH Communications Inc. is a service-oriented business that provides proposal-writing support and training. My business produces revenue and profit by billing clients for my time as a consultant and seminar leader/trainer and by publishing related information.

HRH Communications Inc. is operated as a shareholder-owned corporation. I founded it in 1974 and incorporated it in 1980. HRH Communications Inc. currently has two employees as well as 300-plus customers. We sell our products and services in an international market, the United States, and Canada. I believe we could capture 10 percent of the market. The reason(s) why my clients prefer my services are my national reputation, deriving from my books, and because, unlike other proposal services, I suggest proposal strategies to my clients and help them design the programs they propose to their clients.

As HRH Communications Inc., I sell my services to clients through personal referrals and through the books and other publications that provide visibility on an international scale. I sell my products to clients and subscribers through direct mail, supported by my writing and lecturing. I need to continue to expand that coverage to meet short- and long-range goals. My primary short-range goal is an increase in the number of clients and assignments, which will enable me to raise my daily fees rate. To achieve my primary short-term goal, I must increase leads and sales by raising my visibility further through expanded publications and lecturing activities.

THE BUSINESS

My business provides proposal-writing support and training through direct consulting service and seminars, publishing a newsletter and a number of monographs, and writing books for commercial publication.

My background for providing this service is 35 years of successful experience winning contracts via proposals that have produced more than $360 million worth of contracts for former employers, clients, and my own account. Among the former employers and clients for these services have been RCA, IBM, GE, U.S. Industries, Volt Information Sciences, and Control Data Corporation. I bring to the business and to the services to clients an unusually broad and deep knowledge of marketing to federal government agencies as a former director of marketing and general manager, not only winning but also administering many government contracts.

In general, my clients are companies and others doing business with the federal government and colleges. My proposal service is unique in that I provide more than writing and training in federal procurement; I develop strategies and tactics for clients, often designing the programs to be proposed to their clients. The business earns revenue and profit by billing clients for my time, by selling our publications, and by earning royalties on books written for commercial publishers. Our major costs for providing these services are labor.

HRH Communications Inc.'s office is located in my home, and its mailing address is P.O. Box 1731, Wheaton, MD 20915. My location minimizes overhead costs and reduces my personal salary requirements so as to minimize the burden it places on the business. HRH Communications Inc. currently occupies 400 square feet of space. The major equipment required includes a computer, printer, modem, copier, and fax machine. The principal software required for the computer system is a modern word processor and communications programs. The furniture and fixtures required are ordinary office furniture, shelves, filing cabinet, and minor equipment.

Supplies required are ordinary office supplies and minor equipment—staplers, binders, clips, and other such items. Two telephone lines are required, one for voice, the other for fax and modem. Additional ongoing expenses are subscriptions to CompuServe and other online services and public databases.

HRH Communications Inc. is operated as a shareholder-owned company and we currently have two employees, myself as general manager, and an administrative assistant/bookkeeper. Taxes are handled by a certified public accounting firm.

THE MARKET

HRH Communications Inc. currently has more than 300 customers. I would describe the scope of our market as international, including the United States and Canada. There are an estimated 250,000 potential customers in this market area. I have about fifteen direct competitors who hold approximately 65 percent of the market. I estimate 25 percent of the market is covered by indirect competitors, the providers of temporaries. I feel that we can capture 10 percent of the market within the next four years. My major reason for believing this is my superior reputation as a developer of winning proposals and provider of services far beyond those of most proposal writers.

I derive my information about what services my customers want by doing research in consumer buying trends, keeping up generally with the market through studies of current literature related to this market, and frequent conversation and discussion via computer connections. I perceive an increasing demand for our service. The demand for our product is increasing in size based on the change in population characteristics.

SALES

I currently attract not more than 5 percent of my clients from family and friends, 15 percent from current clients, and 10 percent from cooperative arrangements. The remainder of my business results from following up the many leads that come from those reading my publications and attending my seminars and other presentations from the platform. The most cost effective of these has been referrals, not surprisingly, requiring little effort on my part. (Referrals are all but sold in advance, and generally require minimal effort to close.) On the other hand, the leads resulting from my visibility arising out of my writing and lecturing have been the most productive of good leads, and require some time and effort to close, but the closing rate has been nearly 100 percent.

MANAGEMENT

I am satisfied that the quality of my management has been quite good, although my learning is continuous and management thus continues to improve. I require the books to be kept on a weekly basis—postings to be never more than a week old—and I monitor the books every week to maintain awareness of all sources of income, all sources of expense, the ratios between them, and the linkages between them, as far as such linkages can be established.

The short-term goals for my business are (1) higher daily rate, (2) more clients, and (3) expanded publications. To achieve my first short-term goal I must get more business so I can be more selective and accept only clients who will pay a higher daily fee. To achieve my second short-term goal I must increase my sales promotion, which means more lecturing and wider distribution of my writing. To achieve my third short-term goal I must make my publications profitable enough to employ a writer/editor and increase the direct-mail advertising program.

The long-term goals for my business are to achieve complete solvency and build the publications end of my business into a substantial enterprise that can stand on its own and survive me as a viable, self-supporting business. To do this, I must continue to expand that end of my practice to the point where it can support a staff that will handle the day-to-day functions and details of that business for me.

FINANCIAL CONSIDERATIONS

The following are the financial projections I make for HRH Communications Inc. Profitability will come slowly, with conservative management. The figures are based on the assumption that business will grow slowly and steadily. The figures will be examined every 90 days for the first year, every 180 days in the second year, and every year thereafter, with a view to recasting them as necessary or prudent.

Monthly Expense Forecast—10/20/93

Year Number 1—1st & 2nd Quarters

	Jan	Feb	Mar	Apr	May	Jun
Salaries/Wages	3,000	3,000	3,000	3,000	3,000	3,000
Payroll Taxes	1,100	1,100	1,100	1,100	1,100	1,100
Benefits	450	450	450	450	450	450
Rent/Utilities	325	325	325	325	325	325
Leases	350	350	350	350	350	350
Office Supplies	40	40	40	40	40	40
Advertising	100	100	100	100	100	100
Entertainment	75	75	75	75	75	75
Travel Expense	150	150	150	150	150	50
Communications	175	175	175	175	175	175
Insurance	60	60	60	60	60	60
Legal/Accounting	110	110	110	110	110	110
Other Expenses	50	50	50	50	50	50
TOTALS	5,985	5,985	5,985	5,985	5,985	5,885

Year Number 1—3rd & 4th Quarters

	Jul	Aug	Sep	Oct	Nov	Dec
Salaries/Wages	3,000	3,000	3,000	3,000	3,000	3,000
Payroll Taxes	1,100	1,100	1,100	1,100	1,100	1,100
Benefits	450	450	450	450	450	450
Rent/Utilities	325	325	325	325	325	325
Leases	350	350	350	350	350	350
Office Supplies	40	40	40	40	40	40
Advertising	100	100	100	100	100	100
Entertainment	75	75	75	75	75	75
Travel Expense	50	50	50	50	50	50
Communications	175	175	175	175	175	175
Insurance	60	60	60	60	60	60
Legal/Accounting	110	110	110	110	110	110
Other Expenses	50	50	50	50	50	50
TOTALS	5,885	5,885	5,885	5,885	5,885	5,885

Monthly Expense Forecast—10/20/93

Year Number 2—1st & 2nd Quarters

	Jan	Feb	Mar	Apr	May	Jun
Salaries/Wages	3,500	3,500	3,500	3,500	3,500	3,500
Payroll Taxes	1,250	1,250	1,250	1,250	1,250	1,250
Benefits	490	490	490	490	490	490
Rent/Utilities	343	343	343	343	343	343
Leases	375	375	375	375	375	375
Office Supplies	40	40	40	40	40	40
Advertising	125	125	125	125	125	125
Entertainment	75	75	75	75	75	75
Travel Expense	75	75	75	75	75	75
Communications	200	200	200	200	200	200
Insurance	60	60	60	60	60	60
Legal/Accounting	125	125	125	125	125	125
Other Expenses	50	50	50	50	50	50
TOTALS	6,708	6,708	6,708	6,708	6,708	6,708

Year Number 2—3rd & 4th Quarters

	Jul	Aug	Sep	Oct	Nov	Dec
Salaries/Wages	3,500	3,500	3,500	3,500	3,500	3,500
Payroll Taxes	1,250	1,250	1,250	1,250	1,250	1,250
Benefits	490	490	490	490	490	490
Rent/Utilities	343	343	343	343	343	343
Leases	375	375	375	375	375	375
Office Supplies	40	40	40	40	40	40
Advertising	125	125	125	125	125	125
Entertainment	75	75	75	75	75	75
Travel Expense	75	75	75	75	75	75
Communications	200	200	200	200	200	200
Insurance	60	60	60	60	60	60
Legal/Accounting	125	125	125	125	125	125
Other Expenses	50	50	50	50	50	50
TOTALS	6,708	6,708	6,708	6,708	6,708	6,708

Yearly Expense Forecast—10/20/93

5-Year Projection

	Yr 1	Yr 2	Yr 3	Yr 4	Yr 5
Salaries/Wages	36,000	42,000	46,200	53,130	61,100
Payroll Taxes	13,200	15,000	15,750	16,538	17,364
Benefits	5,400	5,880	6,056	6,238	6,425
Rent/Utilities	3,900	4,116	4,281	4,452	4,630
Leases	4,200	4,500	4,635	4,774	4,917
Office Supplies	480	480	480	480	480
Advertising	1,200	1,500	1,590	1,685	1,787
Entertainment	900	900	1,035	1,087	1,141
Travel Expense	1,100	900	900	900	900
Communications	2,100	2,400	2,592	2,799	3,023
Insurance	720	720	756	794	833
Legal/Accounting	1,320	1,500	1,575	1,654	1,736
Other Expenses	600	600	600	600	600
TOTALS	71,120	80,496	86,450	95,131	104,937

Monthly Income Statement—10/20/93

Year Number 1—1st & 2nd Quarters

	Jan	Feb	Mar	Apr	May	Jun
Sales Forecast	7,500	7,500	8,000	8,000	8,500	8,500
Cost of Sales	1,250	1,250	1,250	1,250	1,250	1,250
Gross Profit	6,250	6,250	6,750	6,750	7,250	7,250
Expenses	5,985	5,985	5,985	5,985	5,985	5,885
Depreciation	1,400	1,400	1,400	1,400	1,400	1,400
Interest	50	50	50	50	50	50
Net Income Before Taxes	–1,185	–1,185	–685	–685	–185	–85

Year Number 1—3rd & 4th Quarters

	Jul	Aug	Sep	Oct	Nov	Dec
Sales Forecast	8,500	8,000	9,000	9,500	9,800	9,800
Cost of Sales	1,250	1,250	1,250	1,250	1,250	1,250
Gross Profit	7,250	6,750	7,750	8,250	8,550	8,550
Expenses	5,885	5,885	5,885	5,885	5,885	5,885
Depreciation	1,400	1,400	1,400	1,400	1,400	1,400
Interest	40	40	40	40	40	40
Net Income Before Taxes	–75	–575	425	925	1,225	1,225

Monthly Income Statement—10/20/93

Year Number 2—1st & 2nd Quarters

	Jan	Feb	Mar	Apr	May	Jun
Sales Forecast	9,800	10,000	10,500	10,500	10,500	10,000
Cost of Sales	1,400	1,400	1,400	1,400	1,400	1,400
Gross Profit	8,400	8,600	9,100	9,100	9,100	8,600
Expenses	6,708	6,708	6,708	6,708	6,708	6,708
Depreciation	1,600	1,600	1,600	1,600	1,600	1,600
Interest	35	35	35	35	35	35
Net Income Before Taxes	57	257	757	757	757	257

Year Number 2—3rd & 4th Quarters

	Jul	Aug	Sep	Oct	Nov	Dec
Sales Forecast	10,000	10,000	11,000	12,000	12,000	12,000
Cost of Sales	1,400	1,400	1,400	1,400	1,400	1,400
Gross Profit	8,600	8,600	9,600	10,600	10,600	10,600
Expenses	6,708	6,708	6,708	6,708	6,708	6,708
Depreciation	1,600	1,600	1,600	1,600	1,600	1,600
Interest	30	30	30	30	30	30
Net Income Before Taxes	262	262	1,262	2,262	2,262	2,262

Monthly Income Statement—10/20/93

5-Year Projection

	Yr 1	Yr 2	Yr 3	Yr 4	Yr 5
Sales Forecast	102,600	128,300	141,130	169,356	211,695
Cost of Sales	15,000	16,800	17,472	18,171	19,079
Gross Profit	87,600	111,500	123,658	151,185	192,616
Expenses	71,120	80,496	86,450	95,131	104,937
Depreciation	16,800	19,200	20,160	21,168	22,226
Interest	540	390	429	472	519
TOTALS	–860	11,414	16,619	34,415	64,933

Appendix

References and Resources

A few suggestions to get help in developing a business plan that will do the job you want it to do for you.

There is no shortage of books on the subject of writing business plans. This is only one of many, although this is a highly specialized book on the subject, a book addressing your special needs as an independent consultant. As I noted in the beginning, almost all books to be found on the subject are focused on the business plan as a tool for raising capital, or as a financial proposal designed to set the mind of a banker or investor at rest. Moreover, most of these books tend to focus on commercial enterprises involving products and, in a great many cases, manufacturing. These subjects are treated as of secondary interest here because the primary interest and central theme is the need of the independent consultant, a vendor of services. Still, some of these other books may be of interest to you, and are therefore listed here for your information, along with other references and resources to help you. A few other sources of help that you ought to know about are listed here also.

BIBLIOGRAPHY

Abrams, Rhonda, M., *The Successful Business Plan: Secrets and Strategies*, Grants Pass, OR: Oasis Press, 1992.

Bangs, David H., Jr., *The Business Planning Guide*, 6th ed., Dover, NH: Upstart Publishing Company Inc., 1992.

Brooks, Julie, and Barry Stevens, *How to Write a Successful Business Plan*, New York: AMACOM, 1991.

Hyypia, Erik, *Crafting the Successful Business Plan*, Englewood Cliffs, NJ: Prentice-Hall, 1992.

Leza, Richard L., and Jose F. Plcencia, *Develop Your Business Plan*, Grants Pass: Oasis Press, 1988.

Luther, William M., *How to Develop a Business Plan in 15 Days*, New York: AMACOM, 1987.

Mancuso, Joseph, *How to Write a Winning Business Plan*, Englewood Cliffs, NJ: Prentice-Hall, 1985.

McLaughlin, Harold J., *Building Your Business Plan: A Step-by-Step Approach*, New York: John Wiley, 1985.

O'Hara, Patrick D., *The Total Business Plan*, New York: John Wiley, 1990.

Porter, Michael, *Competitive Advantage*, New York: Macmillan, 1990.

Rich, Stanley, and David Gumpert, *Business Plans That Win $$$*, New York: Harper & Row, 1985.

Siegel, Eric S., Loren A. Schultz, and Brian R. Ford (edited by David C. Carney), *The Arthur Young Business Plan Guide*, New York: Wiley, 1987.

Siegel, Eric S., Loren A. Schultz, Brian R. Ford, and Jay Bornstein, *The Ernst & Young Business Plan Guide*, New York: Wiley, 1987.

Touchie, Rodger, *Preparing a Successful Business Plan: A Practical Guide for Small Business*, North Vancouver, B.C.: Self-Counsel Press, 1989.

OTHER USEFUL PUBLICATIONS

The *Catalog of Federal Domestic Assistance,* is an annual publication of the federal government, available in Government Printing Office bookstores, listing and describing many grant and other programs to assist small and minority-owned businesses.

Many states have similar programs to aid small and minority-owned businesses in starting. These are generally handled under the aegis of a department in the state capital under such titles as Division of Business Development, Office of Economic Development, Office of Small Business, or similar name. The programs include small direct loans, loan guarantees, preference in awarding state contracts, and other services.

Lesko's Info-Power (Matthew Lesko, Kensington, MD: Information USA, 1990) is a telephone-directory-sized tome that is a mountain of useful information, including guides to all the programs mentioned above.

BUSINESS PLAN CONSULTANTS

There are a number of special consultants who specialize in aiding clients in making financial projections and developing business plans. They can provide services ranging from advising and reviewing your drafts to writing the entire plan for you. Here are two that you should know about:

Linda T. Elkins
3099 Friendship School Rd.
Mechanicsville, MD 20659
(301) 373-3745
CompuServe 72760,3406

Marcia Layton
Layton & Co.
901 East Ave.
Rochester, NY 14607
Tel: (716) 271-4980
Fax: (716) 242-9907
CompuServe 71045,2627

BUSINESS PLAN SOFTWARE

There are a number of computer software programs to help you write a business plan.

Turn Your Idea into a Business Plan, a product of MST Incorporated, is one that is commercially available where software is sold.

Entrepreneur magazine now offers its own business plan software, titled *Developing a Successful Business Plan.*

Bplan is a business plan program that is the joint offering of the National Business Association and the U.S. Small Business Administration (SBA). You can download it from the SBA's own electronic bulletin board system, SBA ONLINE, using either of the following telephone numbers:

9600 baud: 1-800-697-4636
2400 baud: 1-800-859-4636

You can also call 1-800-456-0440 or (214) 991-5381 to reach the National Business Association.

The SBA ONLINE facility offers a great many services and other files. In addition to Bplan.exe, the business plan program referred to above, Cash.Exe, a related program for analyzing your financial position; and PFLoss.Exe, a program to help you develop a profit and loss statement, are just three of many files available there to support your needs in developing your business plan.

The SBA also offers consulting and other direct assistance to small business via the nearest SBA district office listed in your telephone directory.

A FEW USEFUL ADDRESSES

National Federation of Independent Business (NFIB)
600 Maryland Avenue, SW
Washington, DC 20024
A major small business association.

U.S. Small Business Administration
Central (Headquarters) Office
1141 L Street, NW
Washington, DC 20416

Jeffrey Lant
JLA Publications
50 Follen Street
Cambridge, MA 02138
Send for his catalog.

Index

Accounting, 56, 75, 171, 173
  balance sheet, 197
  cost, 57, 168
  Dome® system, 175
  liquidity, 199
  profit and loss (P&L)
    statement, 200
  start-up, 56, 75
Advertising, 120, 137
AIDA, 129
Aronson, Charles, 20

Baruch, Bernard, 171
Business plan
  definition, 7
  elements, 9
  implementation, 42
  mutative nature of, 19
  reasons for writing, 10, 13, 16
  road map, as, 17
  size of, 21
  start-up planning, 47
  writing versus developing/
    building, 18

Business organization
  corporation, 69
  general considerations, 52, 59
  joint venture, 71
  partnership, 65
  sole proprietorship, 63

Capability statements, 137
Capital requirements
  capital items, 176
  financing investment, 188
  marketing costs, 181
  needs list, 176
  start-up, 3, 57
  working capital, 180
Center for Entrepreneurial
  Management, The, 29
Commerce Business Daily, 146
CompuServe, 150
Contingencies, 6, 14, 165
Contracts, 77
Costs
  direct and indirect, 168
  overhead, meaning of, 168

Databases
  basics, 105
  designing, 106
Dba (doing business as), 53, 63
Deere, John, 31
Defining your business
  dependence on clients'
    needs, 31, 39, 81
  evolutionary nature of
    definition, 30
  explaining what you *do*, 35
  general need for, 29
  multiple businesses, 37
Disasters, planning for, 14
Diversification
  ancillary products, 90
  potential for, 5, 9
Dodge Reports, 147
Drucker, Peter, 29

Elkins, Linda, 7, 215

Government contracts, 146

Hershey, Milton, 20
Hoover Company, 31
*How to Write a Winning Business
  Plan,* 29

IBM, 172
Income projections, 6, 186
Insurance, 52, 56, 76
IRS, 119, 136, 174

Jay, Elizabeth M., 19, 20

Layton, Marcia, 8, 215
Legal considerations, 77

Mailing lists
  compiled and response, 141
  compiling your own, 142
Mail order and direct
  marketing, 125, 140, 143
Mallory, P. J., 31
Mancuso, Dr. Joseph R., 29
Markets and marketing
  brokers and subcontracting,
    119, 133, 136, 138 .
  choosing your markets, 81
  clients are individuals, 92
  cold calls, 120, 138
  conventions and trade shows,
    152
  defining your services, 83
  goals, initial, 57
  hospitality suites and other
    sideshows, 158
  importance of, 10
  intelligence, 145, 147, 173
  library for, 150
  marketability, 114, 116
  marketable service, 113
  marketing plan, 82
  marketing databases, 95, 96,
    105, 151
  networking, 122, 139
  niches, 79, 97, 99, 146
  plan and process, 4, 111
  qualifying markets, 97
  research, necessity for, 80
  seminars and workshops, 156
  targeting markets, 104
  testing niches, 99
  understanding what the client
    buys, 87, 131

Maryland Register, 146
Mission statement
    aids to drafting, 28
    definition, basic, 3
    need for accuracy, 25
    objective of, 26
Murphy's Law, 13, 72

Otis, Elisha, 20
Outlines, 2

Papyrus & Silicon, Inc., 19
Positioning
    developing an image, 50
    general, 49
Practice of Management, The, 29
Price Waterhouse, 21
Profiling clients, 40
Profit centers, planning, 5
Proof and promise, 129
Proposals, 137
Publicity and public relations
    general discussion, 122
    newsletters, 185
    press releases, 123, 139
    writing and speaking, 125,
        140, 182

Rates
    elements to consider, 168
    flexibility, need for, 165
    problems in setting, 166
    structure, 5
    "the market," 161
    variables, 159

Sales tools and presentations
    kinds of, 127, 137, 143
    motivation, 128
Sell copy, 143
Specialist as a generalist, 51
Start-up planning
    accounting needs, 56, 75
    costs, 57
    business name, 53
    decisions, 4
    elements of, 47
    incorporation, pros and cons,
        52
    insurance, 52
    minimizing costs, 54
    office location, factors in
        choosing, 52
    organization, choice of 52, 59
    positioning, 49
    short-term goals, setting, 57

Training magazine, 156

Uniform Commercial Code,
    77
U.S. Postal Service, 42

Vernon Saunders Law, 11

"Well begun is half done," 47

User Information

HOW TO MAKE A BACKUP DISKETTE

Before you start to use the enclosed diskette, we strongly recommend that you make a backup copy of the original. Making a backup copy of your disk allows you to have a clean set of files saved in case you accidentally change or delete a file. Remember, however, that a backup disk is for your own personal use only. Any other use of the backup disk violates copyright law. Please take the time now to make the backup copy, using the following instructions:

If your computer has two floppy disk drives:

1.   Insert your DOS disk into drive A of your computer.
2.   Insert a blank disk into drive B of your computer.
3.   At the **A:>**, type **DISKCOPY A: B:** and press Enter. You will be prompted by DOS to place the source disk into drive A.
4.   Place the main disk *Business Plan Guide* into drive A.

Follow the directions on the screen to complete the copy. When you are through, remove the new backup disk from drive B and label it immediately. Remove the original *Business Plan Guide* disk from drive A and store it in a safe place.

Note that this information applies to the cloth edition of this book, ISBN 0-471-59736-8, which contains the diskette.

If your computer has one floppy disk drive and a hard drive:

If you have an internal hard drive on your computer, you can copy the files from the enclosed disk directly onto your hard disk drive, in lieu of making a backup copy, by following the installation instructions below.

INSTALLING THE DISKETTE

The enclosed diskette contains thirty-one individual files in a compressed format. To use the files, you must run the installation program for the disk. You can install the diskette onto your computer by following these steps:

1. Insert the *Business Plan Guide* disk into drive A of your computer. Type **A:\INSTALL** and press Enter.
2. The installation program will be loaded. After the title screen appears, the following menu selections will be listed: Edit Destination Paths, Select Destination Drive, Toggle Overwrite Mode, Select Groups to Install, and Start Installation.
3. The **Destination Path** is the name of the default directory to store the data files. The default directory name is **HOLTZ**. To change this name, press Enter, hit the letter **P**, type in the name of the directory you wish to use, and press Enter.
4. **Select Destination Drive** gives you the option of installing the disk onto a hard disk drive C:\ or the drive you wish to install the files onto.
5. The **Toggle Overwrite Mode** pertains to the user, if you have chosen to give the default directory the same name as an existing directory on your hard drive and you wish to combine the *Business Plan Guide* forms with the other files into that same directory.
6. The **Select Groups to Install** option allows you to install each subdirectory on the disk one by one. The files on this disk are in three different formats: Microsoft Word for Windows, WordPerfect for Windows, and ASCII. To install just one of these three formats, press Enter, hit the letter **G**, select the format you want to install, and hit Enter again. If you wish to

install the entire directory at once, tab down to Start Installation and press Enter.

The files are now successfully installed onto your hard drive. For detailed instructions in using the forms on this disk, load the file Forms.Doc and follow the instructions given there.

READING FILES INTO WORD PROCESSING PROGRAMS

For your convenience, the files on the enclosed diskette are provided in three formats: ASCII, Microsoft Word for Windows, and Word-Perfect for Windows. Because ASCII format is standard format for all DOS computers, a number of different users with different word processing programs can read the disk. Once the files are loaded into your word processor, you can customize them to suit your individual needs. Consequently, regardless of your particular word processing program (WordStar, Microsoft Word for DOS, WordPerfect for DOS, etc.), you can still use the file on the disk. If you have Microsoft Word for Windows or WordPerfect for Windows, you can load files directly into your word processing program without having to convert their formats.

Reading Files into WordPerfect 5.1 for DOS

To read the CLIENT file in WordPerfect, follow these steps:

1. Load the WordPerfect program as normal.
2. When the blank document screen is displayed, press **SHIFT-F10** to retrieve the document.
3. To open the document **CLIENT**, from the subdirectory **HOLTZ**, type the following:

   C:\HOLTZ\CLIENT.WP

4. Press Enter when you have finished typing in the filename.
5. Make your changes and revisions to the document.
6. To print the document, press **SHIFT-F7.**

When you are through editing the file, you can save it under a new file name (to avoid overwriting the original file) before you quit.

Reading the Files into WordPerfect
for Windows

To read the files into WordPerfect for Windows, follow these steps:

1. Load the WordPerfect for Windows program as normal.
2. Select **OPEN** from the **FILE** menu.
3. The **OPEN** dialog will appear, as shown in the figure below. At this box, make the appropriate selections for the drive and subdirectory of the document you want to review. For instance, to open the file **CLIENT** located in the **HOLTZ** subdirectory, you must select the subdirectory.

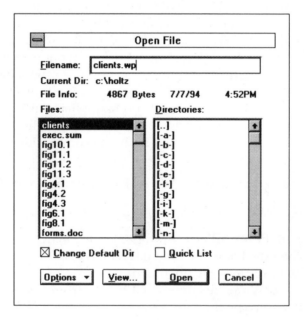

4. Under the **FILES** option on the left side of the dialog box, enter CLIENT as the file name.
5. Make your changes and revisions to the document.
6. To print the file, select **PRINT** from the **FILE** menu.

When you are through editing the file, you should save it under a new file name (to avoid overwriting the original file) before you quit.

Reading the Files into Microsoft Word for Windows

To read the file into Microsoft Word for Windows, follow these steps:

1. Load the Word for Windows program as normal.
2. When the Untitled document is displayed, select **OPEN** form the **FILE** menu.
3. The **OPEN FILE** dialog box will appear, as shown in the figure below. At this box, make the appropriate selections for the drive and subdirectory of the document you want to review. For instance, to open the file **CLIENT** in the **HOLTZ** subdirectory, you must select drive C:\ and the subdirectory **HOLTZ**, and then type **CLIENT** under the file name. Click OK to proceed. The file will immediately load into Microsoft Word for Windows.

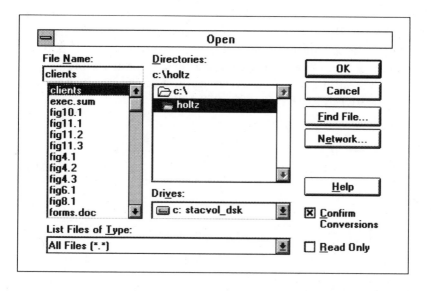

4. Make your changes and revisions to the document.

When you are through editing the file, you should save it under a new name (to avoid overwriting the original file) before you quit.

Reading the ASCII Files into Other Word Processing Programs

To use the ASCII files with other word processing programs, refer to the documentation that accompanies your software. Often, the procedure is similar to those already explained. The two primary steps involved in opening the ASCII files are:

1. Identify the file you want to load from the **HOLTZ** subdirectory and indicate the filename to your word processor.
2. Identify the file as a DOS text file.

After these general steps, most word processing programs will immediately load the file.

USER ASSISTANCE AND INFORMATION

John Wiley & Sons, Inc., is pleased to provide assistance to users of this package. Should you have any questions regarding the use of this package, please call our technical support number, (212) 850-6194, weekdays between 9 A.M. and 4 P.M. Eastern Standard Time.

To place additional orders or to request information about other Wiley products, please call (800) 879-4539.